A READING FROM HOMER

Alma-Tadema

THE STORY OF
THE GREEK PEOPLE

An Elementary History of Greece

BY

EVA MARCH TAPPAN, Ph.D.

Author of "England's Story," "Our Country's Story,"
"American Hero Stories," etc. Editor of
"The Children's Hour"

BOSTON   NEW YORK   CHICAGO   SAN FRANCISCO
HOUGHTON MIFFLIN COMPANY
The Riverside Press Cambridge

The Riverside Press
CAMBRIDGE · MASSACHUSETTS
PRINTED IN THE U.S.A.

IN KINDLY REMEMBRANCE
OF THE ELM STREET GRAMMAR SCHOOL
OF PROVIDENCE, RHODE ISLAND

PREFACE

THE plan of this book is not only to present a simple outline of the chief events in the history of ancient Greece, but also to picture the customs of the people, their manner of living and thinking and feeling. So far as the size and scope of the little volume will permit, the names of those who were masters in art and literature are introduced, not in separate chapters as mere adjuncts to political history, but in their natural connection with the annals of their times, and ever in accordance with Plutarch's dictum, "Often an action of small note, a short saying or a jest, shall distinguish a person's real character more than the greatest sieges or the most important battles."

In treating of the wars of Greece, I have followed their course as briefly as possible, and have given the space often allotted to details of battles to characteristic stories of some of the famous leaders, or a description of some one military operation that illustrates the difference between ancient and modern ways of conducting such affairs. In short, I have used the wars to illustrate the people, and not the people to display the minutiæ of the wars.

The illustrations for the book are intended to put the reader into the spirit of the Greek world, and to aid the imagination in interpreting the text. They have been taken from a great variety of sources, in the majority of cases representing Greek art in the form of architecture, statuary, bas-reliefs, vase-paintings, and coins, which reveal something of the artistic genius and the wonderful versatility of this people.

The never-failing fascination of the study of the Greeks, of their brilliancy of intellect, their love of country, their versatility, even their very faults, must seize upon one who becomes familiar with them in ever so slight a degree. If this little book affords as much pleasure to the reader as its preparation has given to the writer, its existence will be justified.

EVA MARCH TAPPAN.

WORCESTER, MASSACHUSETTS,
     August 15, 1908.

CONTENTS

MAPS

The cover designs represent a Greek chariot (front cover), the Winged Victory (back cover), and the statue of Alexander in the Capitoline Museum at Rome (back edge).

CONTENTS

IMPORTANT DATES IN GREEK HISTORY

B. C.

776 Beginning of First Olympiad.

621 Draco reformed the Athenian laws.

594 Solon reformed the Athenian laws.

509 Clisthenes reformed the Athenian laws.

500–494 The revolt of the Ionians.

490 The battle of Marathon forced Darius to return to Asia.

480 The battles of Thermopylæ and Salamis forced Xerxes to return to Asia.

479 The battle of Platæa freed Greece from the Persians. The battle of Mycale freed the Hellespont and the Ægean islands.

477 The Delian League was formed.

445 The Peace of Pericles gave quiet to Greece.

445–431 The Age of Pericles.

421 The Peace of Nicias ended the Peloponnesian War.

415–413 The Sicilian Expedition.

405 The battle of Ægospotami.

404 The fall of Athens.

401–400 The Retreat of the Ten Thousand.

387 The Peace of Antalcidas ended the Corinthian War.

371 The battle of Leuctra began the downfall of Sparta.

362 The death of Epaminondas at Mantinea ended the supremacy of Thebes.

338 The battle of Chæronea brought all Greece into the power of Philip.

334 Alexander crossed the Hellespont to invade Persia.

323 The death of Alexander and the division of his empire.

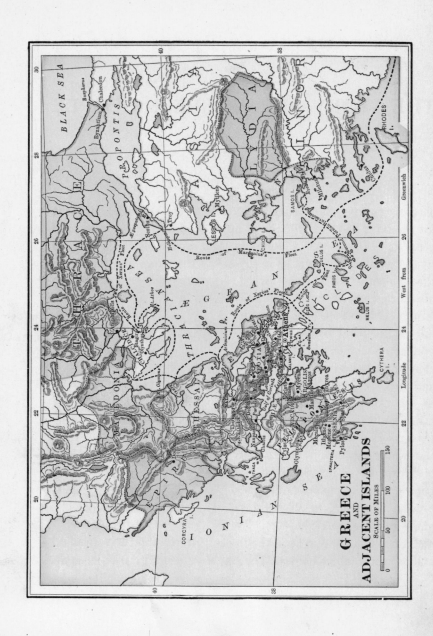

GREECE
AND
ADJACENT ISLANDS

SCALE OF MILES

THE STORY OF THE GREEK PEOPLE

I

IN THE DAYS OF MYTHS

THERE was one thing that must have been especially pleasant for the boys and girls who lived in Greece nearly three thousand years ago. It was that so many of their questions were answered by stories. For instance, if a boy asked the name of a mountain that rose far to the northward, his mother would reply, "That is Mount O-lym'pus. On its summit is the most beautiful palace you can imagine. It is made of clouds, white and rosy and golden, and it is the home of Zeus, King of the Gods. He often calls the other gods to come to him; and then they journey from the earth, the water, and the underworld, and meet in the great hall of the palace. There they feast upon ambrosia and nectar, the Mu'ses sing, and A-pol'lo plays on his lyre. By and by, when the sun sets, they pass through the gates of cloud and return to their homes. The sun is a splendid golden chariot.

The home
of the King
of the Gods

ZEUS, KING OF THE GODS
(In the Vatican Gallery at Rome)

Apollo the Sun-God

Apollo drives it up the sky every morning and down again every afternoon. It is all ablaze with diamonds, and that is why it dazzles your eyes to look at it."

"I should like to drive it," perhaps the little Greek boy would say; and then his mother would tell him of the time when a boy once tried to drive it, and of what happened to him.

Flaxman

"He was called the son of Apollo," the story went, "and his name was Pha′ë-thon. One day a playmate was angry with him and cried out, 'You are nobody! You are not Apollo's son!' Phaëthon did not say a word in reply, but went straight to far-away India, and walked boldly into the palace

APOLLO IN HIS SUN-CHARIOT

of Apollo. The ceilings were of ivory and the doors of silver. At the farther end of the long room stood a throne, which glittered and gleamed and shone like sunbeams sparkling on the water. On this throne sat the Sun-God himself. He wore a crimson robe, and on his head was a crown made of long rays of golden light that flashed and blazed even more brilliantly than the sun at noonday. Phaëthon walked up the room and stood before the throne. Apollo looked kindly upon him and said, 'Tell me who you are and why you have sought me.' Then the boy told the god about his playmate's declaring that he was no child of Apollo. 'And I have come,' he said, 'to beg that if I really am your son, you will give me some proof.'

"Apollo was pleased with the boy's courage. He threw his arms around Phaëthon's neck and said, 'You are my own dear

Story of Phaëthon

Flaxman

THE COUNCIL OF THE GODS
(Zeus is seated on the throne)

son, and to prove it I will give you whatever you ask.' Now, what did the foolish boy ask but permission to drive the fiery chariot for one day. Apollo looked very grave. 'Even the other gods cannot do that,' he said. 'Zeus himself would not attempt it. I beg of you to choose some other gift.' But Phaëthon was bent upon this one thing; and as Apollo had given his word, he had to yield. The headstrong boy sprang into the chariot and seized the reins. The Dawn threw open the eastern gates, all purple and crimson and gold, and the horses galloped up the pathway of the sky.

He drives the sun-chariot

"Any one can guess what happened. A tempest would have been just as easy for the boy to manage as those fiery steeds. He could not even keep them in the road, and they rushed wildly about in one direction and then in another. The light weight of the driver was nothing to them, and the chariot was tossed about like a ship in a storm. Phaëthon did not dare to look at the earth, it was so far below him. He did not dare to look at the sky, it was so full of monsters: the Great Bear, the Little Bear, the Serpent, and the Scorpion. He dropped the reins, and the horses dashed onward more furiously than ever. The fiery chariot swung near and nearer to the earth. The mountains began to smoke, the rivers tried to hide themselves in the sands, the ocean shrank to a lake, and cities burned to ashes. 'Oh, help me, Father Zeus!' cried the Earth. Then Zeus hurled his thunderbolt at Phaëthon, and he fell from the chariot down into the stream E-rid′a-nus. His sisters stood on the bank and wept for him, and by and by they were turned into poplar trees; and even to-day, if you listen to the poplars, you can hear them whispering softly and sadly together of the fate of their lost brother Phaëthon."

His fate

So it was that one story grew out of another, until one almost wonders that the story-tellers ever knew where to stop. If the children asked who made the thick walls of monstrous stones that were old even in those times, the answer was "The Cy′clops"; and then there were stories upon stories of those amazing one-eyed giants. "But where did we ourselves come from?" a child would sometimes ask; and there was a story about that, too. "Once upon a time the people in the world were very wicked," it said, "and Zeus sent a great flood to destroy them. Now Deu-ca′li-on and his wife Pyr′rha were good, and so Zeus promised that they should be saved. After the flood had gone and all the other folk had been drowned, Deucalion and Pyrrha were lonely. 'Let us pray the gods to send people upon the earth,' they said; and they made their way to a temple that was still standing. There was no priest, no fire on the altar, and the floor was deep with mud and stones and rubbish that had been washed in by the flood. Through all this Deucalion and Pyrrha

The Cyclops

Deucalion and Pyrrha

pressed forward to the altar and prayed that the earth might once more be peopled. An answer came: 'Depart from the temple and cast behind you the bones of your mother.' 'Profane the remains of our parents!' Pyrrha cries in horror ; 'Better be alone forever than do that!' Deucalion was silent, but at last he said thoughtfully, 'The earth is the mother of us all, and the

Their prayer answered

Schutzenberger

THE CYCLOPS THROWING IMMENSE ROCKS AT ODYSSEUS'S VESSEL. (See page 21)

stones might be called her bones. I believe the command means that we must pick up stones and cast them behind us. At any rate, let us try and see what will come of it.' They did this, and soon they were no longer alone, for every stone that Deucalion threw became a man, and every one that Pyrrha threw became a woman. One of the sons of the couple was named Hel'len, and we Hel-le'nes are all descended from him. Hellen had two sons and two grandsons. The names of the sons were Æ'o-lus and

Their descendants

Do'rus, and those of the grandsons were I'on and A-chæ'us. That is why there are four tribes of us, — Æ-o'li-ans, Do'ri-ans, I-o'ni-ans, and A-chæ'ans. Other people are barbarians; their talk is all 'ba-ba,' and no one can understand it."

There were almost as many stories of heroes as of gods. The heroes were men who had done some deed of great bravery. They were usually the sons of a god or goddess and a human being. **Theseus, the hero of Athens** Almost every little city of Greece had its hero. The favorite of Athens, for instance, was The'seus; and every Athenian child knew the story of his wonderful exploits, and could tell of the old days when every year Athens had to send seven brave youths and seven fair maidens to Crete (see map, p. 172) to be devoured by the Min'o-taur, a horrible creature with the body of a man and the head of a bull. At last, Theseus, the king's son, insisted upon

THESEUS BEFORE KING MINOS   *Edwards*

being one of the seven youths; and he left Athens in the ship with black sails that carried the terrified young people to their awful fate. Now Theseus had no idea of being eaten by the Minotaur or any other monster,

He plans to kill the Minotaur if sturdy fighting could prevent. He was determined to kill the beast and save his friends or perish; so when the vessel reached Crete and the youths and maidens were brought before the king, he stood out in front of them and said: "King Mi'nos, I demand the privilege of meeting the Minotaur first. I am a prince, and it is my right to be the leader of my people." King Minos smiled disagreeably and said: "Go first if you will, and I will see to it that your people follow you; depend upon that."

Theseus was a brave young fighter, and certainly he would never have run away from the monster; but whether he would have been able to kill it without any help is another question. In some way, however, he and the king's beautiful daughter A-ri-ad'ne had met, and they had fallen in love with each other. Luckily for him, Ariadne knew where to find a sword that in the hands of a valiant man would cut off the Minotaur's ugly head; but there was yet another danger to meet that was even more alarming than an encounter with a monster, and that was the labyrinth which was the

Edwards

THESEUS SLAYING THE MINOTAUR

Ariadne's aid

home of the Minotaur. It had been made by a most skillful workman named Dæd'a-lus, and was so cunningly contrived, with its mazes and windings and turns and twists, that no one who was once within it could ever find his way out. Not even a magic weapon would be of service here; but Ariadne's own bright wits were better than any sword. "Do you hold fast one end of this silken cord," she said to Theseus, "and I will hold the ball as it unwinds. Then when you turn to come back, wind the little cord, and it will lead you straight to me." It all came about as she had said. Theseus killed the monster, then he followed the silken clue till it brought him again to Ariadne. He and the princess and the Athenian youths and maidens sailed away quickly for Athens; and never again did the Athenians pay such a terrible tribute.

King Minos

Minos himself, even though he kept so dreadful a creature as the Minotaur and took the lives of happy boys and girls for its food, was one of the heroes of the Greeks; and they had many legends of the wise laws that he made. They told stories, too, of the danger that sailors used to be in from the pirates, and of how completely King Minos had suppressed them. "He was a mighty king," they would say, "and so just that it is no wonder that after he died he was made one of the judges of the underworld."

Europa and the white bull

Edwards
EUROPA BEING CARRIED AWAY BY THE BULL

King Minos was the son of Zeus and Eu-ro'-pa. There was a story that when Europa was a little girl she went one day to play in a meadow bright with flowers. A beautiful white bull appeared, and at first she was frightened; but he was so gentle and playful that she forgot her fear. She hung wreaths of flowers about his neck, and finally climbed upon his back. Suddenly he turned about, galloped down to the shore, and dashed into the water. He swam far away to the island of Crete. Then he took his own form, and little Europa found that she had been playing with the

King of the Gods, and that he had stolen her away and carried her to this island far over the sea because he loved her so much.

Another hero fully as famous as Theseus was named Œd′i-pus. He lived in Thebes, and just outside of Thebes was a monster quite as horrible as the Minotaur. It was called the Sphinx. It had a woman's head and a lion's body. It lay on a high rock beside the road, and whenever it caught sight of a traveler, it did not come out for a fair fight, but gave him a riddle, and if he could not guess it, then the creature sprang down upon him and devoured him. The riddle was, "What animal is that which in the morning goes upon four feet, at noon upon two, and in the evening upon three?" No one had ever guessed it; but when Œdipus heard it, he answered quietly, "Man, who in childhood creeps on hands and knees, in manhood walks erect, and in old age walks with the aid of a staff." The Sphinx was so angry because the riddle had been guessed that it threw itself down from the rock and perished.

Œdipus and the Sphinx

Perhaps the most famous of all the Grecian heroes was Her′-a-cles, who began to be a hero when he was only a baby of eight months. Two fierce serpents were sent by one of the goddesses to destroy him; but the baby stretched his little arms over the sides of his cradle, seized a snake in each hand, and so squeezed them to death. That was enough to make a legend of, but it was only the smallest of this hero's exploits. One day a command came to him from Zeus, "Go to King Eu-rys′theus and for twelve years obey whatever orders he may give you." Now Eurystheus was an enemy of Heracles, and even so stout-hearted a hero might well have trembled at being in his power for twelve long years. Heracles, however, set out boldly for the kingdom of Eurystheus. He was well armed, for he was a favorite with the

The hero Heracles

THE THREE-HEADED
DOG CERBERUS
(From a bronze statue)

gods, and several of them had given him presents. Apollo had sent him a bow and Her'mes a sword. He-phæs'tos, the lame god who could make all sorts of wonderful things of metal, had made him a golden breastplate. Po-sei'don, ruler of the ocean world, had given him a pair of horses; and A-the'ne, goddess of wisdom and the most skillful weaver in the world, had woven him a robe. He soon reached My-ce'næ, and told King Eurystheus that he was ready to obey his will. Eurystheus knew that his kingdom belonged of right to Heracles, and he sent him on the most dangerous adventures he could hear of, hoping that on some one of them he would be slain. First of all

He kills the Nemean lion

he said: "Go out into the Ne'me-an forest and kill the monstrous lion that is ravaging my country." Heracles set out for the forest, and soon returned with the skin of the lion on his shoulders. The king was so astonished to find that he had such strength, and so afraid Heracles would use it against him, that he had a little room dug underground for a refuge, and covered the walls with heavy plates of brass.

He sent Heracles on other adventures, thinking each time that he had seen the last of him; and when the people began to cry, "The

Crane

HERACLES'S STRUGGLE WITH THE
OLD MAN OF THE SEA

hero is coming, King Eurystheus! Heracles is almost here!" the frightened monarch would slip away to hide in his underground chamber. Twelve exploits, or labors, he demanded of Heracles; The Twelve Labors of Heracles but at last they were completed. The hero had captured a stag with golden horns, a savage boar, and a furious wild bull, and dragged them to the gates of My-cenæ. He had killed all sorts of monsters, one with six legs, and another with nine heads, every one of which had a way of growing out double if any one cut it off; and he had brought up from the under-world a three-headed dog with a dragon tail, to say nothing of such feats as killing a flock of savage birds that ate men and beasts, over-coming the Old Man of the Sea, and holding up the sky for a while that At'las, whose business this was, might bring him some gold-en apples from the Garden of the Hes-per'i-des. Surely, he well earned the reward given him by

Crane

HERACLES AND ATLAS
(Atlas is supporting the sky upon his shoulders)

Zeus, to be carried to the heavens and placed among the gods.

Eurystheus pursued the children of Heracles and drove them out of the kingdom. He even made war upon Athens because The Hera-clidæ driven out of the kingdom that city had received them. He was slain in this war; and then the kingdom belonged to Hyl'lus, eldest son of Heracles; that is, it would belong to him if he could take it. It seemed as if there would have to be a great deal of hard fighting before the matter was settled; but finally both sides agreed that Hyllus and the champion among his enemies should meet in single combat. If Hyllus won, he was to have the kingdom; but if the champion won, Hyllus and his friends must wait for a hundred years before trying again to seize the crown. All the men on both sides stood watching eagerly; but soon the sons of Heracles were sad enough, for Hyllus was slain. They kept their promise, and neither they nor their children nor their grandchildren made any attempt to seize the kingdom. At last, however, the hundred years had come to an end, and the three great-great-grandsons of Heracles, or the Her-a-cli′dæ as they were called, set out with their friends **The Return of the Hera-clidæ** to regain the lands that belonged to their family. This time they were successful, and their expedition is called the Return of the Heraclidæ.

SUMMARY

In early Greece many questions of children were answered by stories. Some of the stories were: —

The Home of the King of the Gods.
Phaëthon and the Chariot of the Sun-God.
The Cyclopean Walls.
Deucalion and Pyrrha.
Theseus and the Minotaur.
Europa and the White Bull.
Œdipus and the Sphinx.
Heracles and his Twelve Labors.

SUGGESTIONS FOR WRITTEN WORK

One of the poplar trees by Eridanus tells a child the story of Phaëthon.

Europa tells about her playing with the white bull.

Write a story of some one of Heracles's exploits.

II

IN THE DAYS OF MYTHS (*Continued*)

WITH hundreds of such stories as these, the children hardly needed books of fairy tales, even if there had been any in those days. But I fancy that the tales they liked best were of wonderful voyages said to have been made long before their fathers or grandfathers or great-grandfathers could remember. One of these was known as the Quest of the Golden Fleece. This fleece had been hung in a grove in Col'chis (see map, p. **195**), a country a long way from Greece; and more than one young hero had said to himself, "How I wish I could win it!" The difficulty was that it was guarded by a fire-breathing dragon, which never fell asleep for even a moment; and many a brave man, who was ready to fight with two or three or even four or five stout warriors, did not like to run the risk of being turned into a cinder.

The Quest of the Golden Fleece

Now there was a young man named Ja'son, who was heir to a kingdom in Thes'sa-ly. His uncle Pe'li-as was to hold it for him until the boy had grown up; and when Jason, a brave, stalwart young man, appeared at court and said that he had come to take possession of his throne, the uncle set his wits to work to find some way of continuing to hold it. He pretended to be very ready to give it up. "But you are a young man," said he, "and before you settle down to the cares of a kingdom, should you not like to win a little glory? How would it please you to engage in some wonderful adventure, so that your subjects may tell of your achievements hundreds of years after you are dead?"

Jason claims his throne

Edwards

JASON CLAIMING HIS KINGDOM

The Argonauts

Pelias saw Jason's eyes sparkle, and the wily king then spoke of the quest of the fleece as the most glorious adventure one could engage in. Jason was delighted at the thought, and set to work at once to prepare a vessel that would hold fifty men. This of itself was an amazing undertaking, for the boats of those days were only little canoes made by hollowing out trunks of trees. The vessel was named the Ar'go, for Ar'gus, its builder, and the fifty young men who sailed away in it were called the Ar'go-nauts.

When they were ready, the shores were crowded with people watching to see them start. King Pelias was there, of course. He pretended to be troubled because his nephew was going on so dangerous an expedition; but all the time he was saying to himself, "He'll never, never, never come back, and the kingdom will be mine."

The fifty young men were soon out of sight, and many were the adventures that they met before they came to the kingdom of Their arrival in Colchis Colchis. Once there, Jason went straight to King Æ-e'tes and told him that he had come for the fleece. Now, in order to get this treasure, Æetes had murdered the one to whom it belonged, and he had no idea of losing it. He was as wily an old ruler, however, as King Pelias, and he did not refuse to give it up. "It is only fair, though," he said to Jason, "that you should do two little favors for me first, and then you are welcome to fight the dragon and carry away the fleece — and the grove, too, if you will." The two little favors were to yoke to the plough two fire-breathing bulls, and to

THE ARGONAUTS IN THE ARGO

Edwards

The request of King Æetes

plant the teeth of a dragon that Cad'mus, a hero who lived long before this time, had slain.

Just as in the case of the Minotaur, so there was here also a princess who was much in love with the hero of the adventure, and she gave Jason a charm that made the bulls as gentle as

Medea's aid

lambs. They were soon yoked to the plough, and Jason was ready for the second trial, the sowing of the dragon's teeth. He knew very well what would happen, but he went on as quietly as if he

JASON AND MEDEA

had been sowing corn. In less time than it takes to tell the story, every tooth had sprung up, not as corn, however, but as an armed man, who stood for a moment growling savagely and looking about for some one to kill. The instant the men caught sight of Jason, they drew their swords and rushed fiercely upon him. Before this the princess Me-de′a had told

him how to save himself, and so he caught up a stone and threw it among the furious warriors. Each one thought his neighbor had struck him, and in a minute they were all fighting wildly. In another minute every one of them was dead.

Jason captures the Golden Fleece

After Jason's practice with the fire-breathing bulls, he might have been able to get the better of even the dragon that guarded the fleece; but he thought it was better to sprinkle it with the magic potion that Medea had prepared. In a moment it was sound asleep, and it was the easiest thing in the world to take down the fleece from the tree on which it hung. He was too wise to go to King Æetes to say farewell, and he hastened away to his own kingdom as fast as oars and sails would carry him.

The Trojan War

Another old story, the most famous of all, is of the war with Troy. It began because of Hel′en, the most beautiful woman in Greece. She had a great many suitors, and her father made them all take an oath that whomsoever she chose for a husband they would protect and help if he was ever in trouble. She chose Men-e-la'us, king of Spar'ta, and for several years all went on happily. At length Par'is, son of the king of Troy, came to visit Sparta, and when he went home he carried Helen with him. Now was the time for the other princes to help Menelaus, but some of them would far rather have stayed at home. O-dys'-seus, for instance, did not wish to go, and he thought he could escape by pretending to be insane. He yoked an ox and an ass

Cause of the war

together, and began to sow salt. He was soon found out, however; for when his baby son was laid on the ground before the plough, he turned aside much too carefully for an insane man.

It took two years to build the ships and make ready; but at length the Greeks had crossed the sea and were encamped before the walls of Troy. Their leader was Menelaus's brother, Ag-a-mem'non. For nine years the war went on; but the Greeks could not capture Troy, and the Tro'jans could

HELEN OF TROY   *Leighton*

The Greeks besiege Troy

not drive them away. There were the most valiant of heroes on both sides; and the gods, too, took part in the struggle. Aph-ro-di'te favored the Trojans, and with good reason, for her son

Æ-ne'as was one of the bravest among them. Moreover, she persuaded A'res, the god of war, to help them. Apollo stood first with one party and then with the other. Athene, goddess of wisdom, and He'ra, the wife of Zeus, hated the Trojans, and especially Paris; for he had once given the prize for beauty to Aphrodite rather than to either of them. Poor Zeus had a hard time in his beautiful Olympian palace, for Aphrodite would come to him crying, and beg him to be good to her beloved Æneas; and no sooner had he comforted her with kindly promises than his wife Hera would play some trick to turn his eyes away from Troy and then the Greeks were sure to win a victory or kill some famous Trojan champion

PLAN OF THE SIEGE OF
TROY

During all the years of fighting the Trojans had never really believed that they would lose their city because it was protected by an image of Athene which was said to have fallen from the sky. The Greeks knew of this image

They felt sure that if they could get possession of it, Troy would fall; and at last the crafty Odysseus and his friend Di-o-me'des succeeded in stealing it. Still Troy did not yield, and the fighting went on.

Flaxman

ATHENE AND HERA GOING TO ASSIST THE GREEKS
IN A BATTLE WITH THE TROJANS

After a while the Greeks began to build an enormous wooden horse on the plain just outside the city walls. They contrived to spread the story that they had given up the siege and were going home; then they sailed away, leaving the great horse behind them.

The Trojans could not find out their reason for building the monster; but while they were talking about it and gazing at it, some shepherds brought into the town a young Greek named Si'non, whom they had captured. He told a pitiful story.

THE WOODEN HORSE OF TROY

Cleyn

GREEK SOLDIER

He said that Odysseus hated him, and had induced the Greek soothsayer to declare that he must be put to death as a sacrifice for their safe return to Greece. He had escaped and hidden in a swamp till the Greeks had gone.

The Trojans were ready to be kind to any man whom Odysseus hated. King Pri'am at once ordered him to be freed from his bonds, and bade him forget the Greeks and become a Trojan.

Sinon's treachery

"But tell us why that monster of a horse was built," he said; and Sinon declared that it was a sacrifice to Athene because she was angry with them for touching her statue with bloody hands. "It was made too large to pass through your city gates," he explained, "for they knew that if it was once within your walls, it would protect you, and victory would come to you instead of to the Greeks."

The Trojans believed every word that Sinon said. They tied ropes to the huge figure and began to drag it into the city. They even tore down a place in the walls to make a passage for it. That night the treacherous Sinon opened a door in the body of the horse, and a party of armed Greeks hidden within let down a rope and slid noiselessly to the ground. The Trojans were asleep, and it was an easy matter to kill the watchmen and throw open the gates to the other Greeks; for they had not sailed to Greece, but had only hidden behind a little island a few miles away.

The fall of Troy

HOMER RECITING HIS POEMS   *Gérard*

This is the famous story of the fall of Troy, or Il'i-um. It has

come down to us in a grand old poem called the Il′i-ad, so we can
read it in the very words in which it was known to the Greeks.
The Iliad tells the tale as far as the death of Hec′tor, a brave
Trojan warrior who was slain by A-chil′les; but the story of the

wooden horse comes
from another great
poem, the Æ-ne′id,
which was written by
the Latin poet Vir′gil.
The Greeks believed
that the Iliad was
composed by a blind
poet named Homer,
who was born on the
island of Chi′os, and
who wandered about

Burne-Jones

CIRCE

(She is represented as preparing the magic drink that turned men into beasts)

the land reciting or chanting his poems. He was a beggar, and
yet he was a welcome guest at the house of every chieftain, for
at the feasts he could play on his four-stringed harp and sing of
the wonderful deeds of the olden time. He composed another
poem, the Od′ys-sey, which is about the wanderings of Odysseus; for the baby that had been laid in front of the plough had
become a stalwart young man before the gods would permit the
hero to return to his home. Odysseus had most amazing adventures. He visited the land of the Lotus-eaters. Those who ate
of the lotus forgot all about home and friends, and Odysseus had
to drag some of his men away by main force. He was shut up in
a cave by one of the Cyclops; he stopped at the island of the
magician Cir′ce, who turned men into beasts; he sailed cautiously
between the two monsters, Scyl′la and Charyb′dis. One of the

His return home

sea-nymphs promised to make him immortal if he would only forget his home and remain on her island; but he was still longing for his wife and his son on the island of Ith'a-ca, and finally he succeeded in making his way thither. He revealed himself to his son, and together they punished the suitors who had been wasting his property and troubling his wife.

Origin of the myths

Schutzenberger
THE RETURN OF ODYSSEUS
(The court of the ancient Greek house is shown. See page 24)

These old stories are well worth knowing, just because they are good stories; but besides this each one of them has some bit of truth for a starting-point. The minds of the Greeks were full of poetic fancies, and it was easy to turn the memory of a hot, dry summer, for instance, that ended with thunderstorms, into the story of Phaëthon; or the account of some piratical voyage into the poetry of the golden fleece.

Meaning of these myths

The story of Theseus probably means that at some time tribute was paid to Crete by the Athenians. The return of the Heraclidæ must refer to the times when the Dorians pushed their way into the Pel-o-pon-ne′sus and got possession of the greater part of the peninsula.

Even with the help of these stories, we do not know nearly so much about the early history of Greece as we should like. We can, however, be almost sure of a few facts, namely: —

That the Greeks belonged to the great Ar′y-an race that used to live in central Asia; that they came to Greece in small bands of immigrants; that they were divided into four tribes, Æolians, Dorians, Ionians, and Achæans; that the Dorians pushed down into the Peloponnesus and crowded out many of the Achæans; that these Achæans made their way to the north and drove out the Æolians, who then crossed the Ægean Sea and founded colonies on the shores of Asia Minor; that they were followed by the Ionians, and finally by some of the Dorians, who did not find room enough in the Peloponnesus; that there was fighting at intervals between Greece and Asia Minor for hundreds of years, until Greece was finally conquered by Alexander, king of Mac-e-do′ni-a. This, however, was only three centuries before Christ.

Facts about the Greeks

SUMMARY

One of the best-known myths is the tale of the Golden Fleece.

The most famous stories are of the Trojan War, which is told partly in Homer's Iliad and partly in Virgil's Æneid; and of the wanderings of Odysseus, told in Homer's Odyssey.

These are myths, but every myth is founded upon some bit of truth, and, therefore, we may be sure of a few facts about the early history of Greece.

SUGGESTIONS FOR WRITTEN WORK

Describe the grove and the Golden Fleece.

Sinon tells the Greeks what he plans to do.

Describe the coming of Homer to the house of a chieftain.

III

HOW THE EARLY GREEKS LIVED

As has been said before, we do not know very much about what happened to the Greeks in the early times, what wars they fought or what tribes they overcame. We do know, however, how they lived, how they amused themselves, and what they thought on many subjects; and this is far more interesting.

The house of a prince

If you had gone to the home of one of the Greek princes in the early days, you would have come first to a high, thick stone wall, with a strong folding-door. When the door was drawn back and you stepped into the court, a big dog would have sprung out of

DOOR OF A HOUSE

his kennel to see whether he, as well as his master, thought you ought to be admitted. If the master was an especially wealthy prince, he might not have a real dog, but rather the image of one, made of gold or silver.

Close to the gates were benches of stone, carved and polished, where people might sit and talk. In the farther part of the court were stables for the horses and oxen and carriages, and also places for pigs and geese and sheep. The court was large enough for a garden, and even an orchard of pear, apple, fig, and olive trees. Indeed, the house with its court and heavy wall was almost like a fortified village. There was a fountain, of course; and with plenty of water, with flocks and herds, and the grain that was kept in store, such a place could have endured quite a long siege without being starved out.

The house itself had porticoes and pillars and many rooms. There was a second story; and here was a storeroom where the **Treasures of the early Greeks** treasures of the prince were kept. There was no money in it, for the early Greeks did not coin money; they counted the value of things in oxen. A slave was worth from four to twenty oxen, for instance. There was plenty of the precious metals in other forms than money, however, for there were vases, cups, bowls, and other dishes of solid gold and silver. They were of graceful, beautiful shapes, for the Greeks so liked to have everything around them pleasing to the eye that even the coarsest earthen dish often had a border pretty enough for a silver vase; perhaps a dance of fauns was painted on

ANCIENT GREEK VASE

it, or a foot-race, or Jason and his fifty companions setting out on the quest of the golden fleece. In this storeroom there were, too, great wooden chests ornamented with gold and silver and ivory; and in these were kept costly robes and cloaks and carpets and fine linen and woven coverings for the benches and beds. There were bracelets and necklaces of many sorts; and, more precious than all these, there were the swords and spears and knives and **Their weapons** bows and arrows with which the prince and his men would protect their treasures if the house was attacked by enemies. The metal used in making weapons was sometimes bronze and sometimes copper; but the copper was hardened in some way that we do not understand.

The princes who lived in such houses had slaves, some of whom had been captured in war and some stolen away from their homes; but the masters were no more afraid to work with their

THE VAPHIO CUPS
(Masterpieces of early Greek art.   They are made of gold and are 3¼ inches high)

**The life of
the early
Greeks**
own hands than the poor people who lived in huts. Homer tells us that the royal Odysseus made his own bedstead; and one of the poet's prettiest stories is of the fair young princess Nausic′a-ä setting out with her maidens and a basket of lunch for the river bank to do the washing of the family, and then playing ball with the maidens as merrily as any girl who was not a princess might have done. It is a pity that we cannot know what was

DESIGN ON ONE OF THE VAPHIO CUPS
(It represents a wild bull hunt)

**Their simple
food**
in that picnic basket, full of "all manner of food to the heart's desire," as Homer puts it. There must have been dainties made especially to please the young girls, for at the feasts there seems to have been only the simplest of food, hardly more than bread and meat. The Greeks did not like to be hungry any better than

other people; but when they went to a feast, they thought less about the food they were to eat than about the people with whom they should talk.

If we could have looked in upon one of their banquets, we should have seen a room full of guests, with servants placing among them little tables only large enough for one person. A chair was put before each table, and the guests took their seats. The servants brought them silver bowls of water, in which they washed their hands. Then great joints were borne in and laid before the carver, who cut the meat into mouthfuls, a very necessary thing to do, for there were no forks in those days, and if people ate at all they had to eat with their fingers. A dish of meat was placed before each guest, and then baskets of bread were passed around. The drink was wine, but often three times as much water as wine was poured into the cup. It was always passed to the oldest first, even if he was only a common man and young princes were among the guests. To drink too much was a disgrace; for to the Greeks a drunken man was a most disgusting object, and there was nothing more insulting than to accuse a man of having ever taken too much wine. The bard was present, of course, and he was always a welcome guest. This is the way Homer describes his reception:—

"The page drew near, leading the honored bard. The muse had greatly loved him, and had given him good and ill; she took

The banquet

The Greeks were temperate

GREEK GIRLS PLAYING BALL

Leighton

The bard away his eyesight, but gave delightful song. Pon-ton′o-us placed
for him among the feasters a silver-studded chair, backed by a

lofty pillar, and hung
the tuneful lyre upon
its peg above his head,
and the page showed
him how to reach it
with his hands. By
him he set a tray
and a good table, and
placed thereon a cup
of wine to drink as
need should bid."

A GREEK BARD   *Flaxman*

If a stranger ap-
peared and asked for
food, he was treated as a friend, and no one questioned who
he was or whither he was going, until he had eaten all that he
wanted. Even if a man's worst enemy
came to his door with an olive branch
in his hand, or made his way into the
house and knelt at the hearth, he must
have food and shelter, and no one was
allowed to do him harm.

The children of the early times did
The children in early times not go to school. Why should they when
the chief thing for a girl to learn was
how to manage the house as her mother
did; and the chief thing for a boy to learn was how to do what

A GREEK GIRL SPINNING

his father did? Therefore the girl followed her mother about the
house, learning how it should be cared for, and how to teach the

slaves to do their work. She must learn to spin and weave, of course, and to sing and dance. The boy, too, was taught singing and dancing; but he must also learn to care for the herds and flocks, to cultivate the land, and to use weapons. There was no need of studying reading or writing, for there was little if any to study. All the arithmetic that was necessary could be learned from counting the flocks. As for history, that consisted of myths and legends, which were no harder to remember than so many fairy tales. Geography, too, must have seemed almost like a fairy tale; for the early Greeks thought the earth was a plain, around which the ocean, a broad river, was ever flowing. Beyond this ocean-stream was darkness, and no one knew what fearful monsters. The sky was two mighty domes, a bright one that was overhead by day, and a dark one that shut down at night. Greek children played games, of course, and some of them were much the same as those played to-day. One was called "Five Pebbles." In this the child tossed up five little pebbles and tried to catch as many as possible on the back of his hand. Those that fell to the ground he might pick up, but in so doing he must not drop the others.

The boy's education

A GREEK BOY

The Greeks enjoyed life, and looked upon death as putting an end to all their joys. They believed that they would live forever, but they did not expect to be happy in the after life. Great heroes, to be sure, were borne to a beautiful place called the E-lys′ian Fields, which lay far to the west, close beside the ocean-stream. Homer said of it, "No snow is here, no winter long, no rain; but the loud-blowing breezes of the west the Ocean-stream sends up to bring men to cool-

The Elysian Fields

ULYSSES AND NAUSICAÄ
(Showing the happy outdoor life of the Greeks)

Gleyre

ness." There the heroes went on with whatever they had liked best to do on earth, and there they enjoyed all sorts of pleasures; but no such happiness was in store for common men. They **Hades** expected to be sent to a sad and gloomy place called Ha'des. There they would remember the light of the sun and long to see it again; they would remember their homes and friends, but almost as if they were dreaming. Nothing would seem real, and all things would be dull and cheerless. They would wander about like shadows in the dismal twilight forever, with nothing to enjoy and nothing to hope for.

As the Greeks did not expect any happiness after death, they

were all the more eager to have as much as possible while they How the Greeks thought of their gods
lived. They thought the gods had power to give them whatever
they wanted, provided the Fates did not forbid; therefore they
worshiped them in order to win favors for themselves. They did
not often think of the gods as being better than men, but only
as being more powerful. Parents did not say to their children, "Zeus is good, and therefore you must try to be
like him"; they said, "Zeus can give you what you
want, and so you must offer up a sacrifice to him."
They believed that one god had the power to give
safe returns from journeys; another, recovery from
illness; another, victory over enemies; and therefore they prayed to the one whom they thought
most likely to grant the special favor that they
wished.

HADES, RULER OF THE LOWER WORLD

(The Lower World was also called Hades)

How to please the gods, and so get what they
wanted, was an important matter. The Greeks
who lived at the time when Homer is thought to
have sung used to talk together of the golden
days when the gods walked about among men,
doing them harm sometimes, to be sure, but often
helping and advising them. They no longer expected to meet How to please the gods
gods and goddesses when they were walking about in the forests,
and to learn their commands and feelings they watched for signs
and tokens. If a sacrifice was offered to Zeus, the falling of
a thunderbolt meant that he was pleased and would grant the
prayer. A sudden tempest showed that he was angry. Birds that
flew far up in the air were supposed to have learned the secrets of
the gods, and therefore their movements were closely watched.

There was a surer way, however, of learning the will of the

Oracles gods, and that was by going to an oracle, or place chosen by them to make their will known. There were many oracles in Greece, usually situated in wild, gloomy spots, in the depths of a forest or among the most jagged rocks and precipices. The oldest oracle was that of Zeus, in the narrow valley of Do-do′na in E-pi′rus. Whoever wished to consult it first made gifts to the priests. They offered up sacrifices, and then listened to hear what answer would

Schmalz

GREEK WORSHIP
(The procession is approaching the statue of a god)

come. The only sounds heard were the cooing of doves, the rustling of the breeze among the leaves of the sacred oaks, and the murmuring of the spring at their foot; but the priests claimed that they could understand these sounds and interpret them. **The Dodona** No question was too important to be carried to Dodona, and none **oracle** was too trivial. Heracles himself was said to have gone to ask when his labors would be at an end; and one troubled householder went to inquire whether his vanished coverlets and pillows were lost or had been stolen.

The most famous oracle was that of Apollo, at Del'phi in Pho'cis. Here was a deep cleft in the rocks of Mount Par-nas'sus, and from a fissure rose a stupefying vapor. The priestess was placed on a tripod over this fissure, and soon the gas made her half unconscious. Then the priests noted all her mutterings, and interpreted them for the one who had come to consult the oracle. **The Delphian oracle**

These priests must have contrived to know a good deal about what was going on in the world, for their replies were exceedingly keen and shrewd. They were especially skillful in so framing their answers that they could be read with opposite meanings; and if **Wisdom of the oracles**

the event did not result as the questioner expected, they could say that it was his own fault for not reading the answer aright. For instance, King Crœ'sus of Lyd'i-a asked, "If I invade Persia,

THE VALE OF DELPHI
(From a photograph)

shall I succeed?" The answer was, "If you invade Persia, you will overthrow a mighty empire"; and so he did, but it was his own, and not the Persian, as he had expected. The question was once asked, "Is there any man who is wiser than Soc'ra-tes?" and the answer was "No." When the philosopher heard of this, he said, "The oracle is right. None of us know what is truly good **Socrates and the oracle** and honorable; but I see my ignorance, while they do not see theirs; therefore I am wiser than they."

Wherever there was an oracle, there a temple was built. Suppliants always gave generously to these temples, and therefore they became very rich, especially that at Delphi. All Greeks looked upon the oracles as sacred, and lest some harm should come to the temples with their masses of treasure, groups of cities began to unite that they might protect them if need should **The amphic-** arise. These unions were called am-phic'ty-o-nies, or "groups of **tyonies** neighbors." The Delphic amphictyony was, as one would expect, the strongest of all. This was made up of twelve tribes, all of whom dwelt north of the Isthmus of Corinth. They agreed to protect the temple of Apollo at Delphi, and to punish whoever might attempt to steal its treasures. They also took care of the roads that led to the shrine; and if any one ventured to annoy the suppliants who were on their way to it, he had the whole Delphic amphictyony to reckon with. In spite of this union, the tribes expected to make war upon one another if they chose; but they agreed that when they fought, they would not destroy one another's towns or try to cut them off from running water; and even this was a vast improvement on the usual way of fighting in those times, when it was thought fair to get the better of an enemy in any way possible.

The amphictyonies did much to make the Greeks feel that they were of one race, and that even if they did quarrel, they all belonged to the same family. This feeling was strengthened by their speaking the same language. A third bond that united them more closely with one another than with the "barbarians" **The games** was the "games," in which Greeks alone were allowed to contend. Even in Homer's time, and no one knows how much

AN ANCIENT GREEK TEMPLE, RESTORED

earlier, the Greeks believed that the gods liked to watch athletic contests; and, therefore, at any large festival in honor of a god the races were as important as the sacrifices. Four of these festivals became famous, and the one held at O-lym'pi-a in honor of Zeus was the most renowned of all. In later times, as will be seen farther on, many different kinds of contests were practiced; but the foot-race was always the chief event, and in earlier days it was the only one. In 776 B. C. the Greeks began to record the names of the victors. This date marks the end of the legendary times and the beginning of the real history of Greece.

Beginning of known Greek history, 776 B. C.

SUMMARY

The home of a Greek prince in early times was almost like a fortified village. The house contained many beautiful and costly articles and also weapons.

The feasts were simple, and the bard was ever a welcome guest.

Children were taught to do what their parents did.

The Greeks expected to live forever, but did not expect happiness in the after life. They worshiped the gods in order to win favors for themselves. The oracles were believed to reveal the will of the gods. The most famous was at Delphi. The temples at the oracles were very rich.

Three bonds uniting the Greeks were, (1) the amphictyonies; (2) the language; and (3) the games.

SUGGESTIONS FOR WRITTEN WORK

Describe a visit to a Greek prince.
Write a story of a child's offering a sacrifice to Zeus.
Describe (from a picture) a Greek vase or cup.

IV

HOW THE SPARTANS BECAME POWERFUL

IF the geography of Greece had been different, the story of the Greeks might have been quite unlike what it was. The land was

Why the Greeks loved their homes and also adventure

made up of mountain ranges and fertile valleys. It was not easy to cross these mountains, and therefore there were almost as many tiny kingdoms as there were valleys. The people of each loved their own valley and their own customs, and the Greeks might have been contented to stay at home if it had not been for the sea; but the sea was on three sides of them, pushing its way into the land in sharp, narrow bays. Go where they would, so long as the Greeks did not leave Greece, they could never be more than forty miles from the ocean. The valleys said, "Stay," but the ocean was ever tempting them to go.

There were not many good harbors on the western coast of Greece, but there were plenty of them on the eastern. Moreover, when the Greeks stood on the eastern shore and looked over the water, they could see islands far and near, every one inviting them to visit it. When they came to one there were always others a little farther on; therefore it was easy to make their way across the Æ-ge'an Sea to Asia Minor. There was reason, then, why the Greeks should have loved, not the whole country, but each tribe its own little corner; and also why they should have liked to make voyages and found settlements in other lands, especially to the eastward.

The many islands led to colonization

Greece was a very beautiful country. The sea was blue and sparkling; the mountains were not always covered with

ISLANDS NEAR GREECE
(From a photograph)

green forests, but the hard rock of their summits made sharp, clear outlines of red and gray against the sky. The rivers flowed

The beauty of Greece

swiftly, and often they sank out of sight in a chasm or underground passage, and came bubbling up again in some other place. It is little wonder that the Greeks fancied they were alive, and used to offer sacrifices at the building of a bridge, that the god of the stream might not be angry. In some parts of the land there were fine old forests of oak and beech and chestnut; there were olives and fig trees; there were flowers of many kinds, — roses, violets, crocuses, geraniums, daffodils, heliotropes, and anemones. Along the rivers grew oleanders; not little shrubs, but real trees with their rose-colored blossoms reflected in the water. It was all so beautiful that the Greeks could hardly have helped loving beauty. In At'tica a range of mountains kept off the chill of the northern winds, while the sea-breezes

TYPICAL GRECIAN SCENERY
(The plain below Delphi)

from the south and east made the country cooler in the summer and warmer in the winter. Much of Greece was like Attica in having a bright, clear sky, and being warm enough for people to spend the greater part of their time out of doors.

The Return of the Heraclidæ

It is little wonder that when the Dorians, who lived far to the north, heard of this beautiful country, they were eager to dwell in it, and journeyed southward to take it away from the people who already held it, the Achæans and the Ionians. This is the meaning of the story of the return of the Heraclidæ. The Achæans and the Ionians were not strong enough to drive away the Dorians, and therefore many of them left the country and made colonies on the coast of Asia Minor and the islands near it. This was not done all at once; the emigration was probably going on for many years. At length, reports came back to Greece that the lands to which the colonists had gone were more fertile than even the Peloponnesus; and then some of the Dorians themselves began to found colonies on the coast of Asia Minor and in Crete.

When the Dorians came to the Peloponnesus, they found them- The Dorians settle in the Peloponnesus
selves in a rather difficult position. They were hardy and warlike,
and they succeeded in founding a number of settlements; but
there were ten times as many of the earlier settlers as of themselves. The chief town of the Dorians was Sparta, in La-co′ni-a;
but even after they had conquered the country, they were in
constant danger from the old inhabitants. Of these there were

SPARTA

two classes: the Per-i-œ′ki, who were allowed to keep their The Periœki and the Helots
property, but could have nothing to say about making the laws;
and the He′lots, or slaves. It is said that the Helots had belonged
to the town that had held out longest against the Spartans, and
that the conquerors had declared in their anger that the Helots
should be their slaves forever. These Helots so hated their masters that people used to say, "A Helot will gladly eat a Spartan

raw." The Spartans, on their part, were glad to have slaves to do their work; but they were always a little afraid the Helots would unite against them, and they did not hesitate to put to death any that seemed likely to become leaders of their people.

Laconia was an easy country to defend, for there were mountains on the east, north, and west. On the east and north there were only two or three passes through which an army could be led without great difficulty, and on the west was the conquered land

LYCURGUS OFFERING TO GO INTO EXILE

of Mes-se'ni-a. Sparta, then, was a natural fortress. Still, the Spartans were but a small tribe in the midst of enemies, and the question was how they should make sure of never being over-come by their neighbors. They con-cluded that the only way to do this was to make their whole tribe into an army. Of course the imaginative Greeks had a story

about how this was done. They said that early in their history a man named Ly-cur'gus was made guardian of their baby king. The people paid him so much honor that his enemies were jealous and spread the rumor that he intended to seize the crown. He was indignant, and said to the people, "I will leave the land, and stay away until the king is grown up." He loved his country, however, and in all the years that he was in exile he was visiting different kingdoms to see what had given them power and what had weakened them. Every little while the Spartans sent to urge him to return; and at last he came, his mind full of plans for making his country powerful. He had been to Delphi on his way, and had asked Apollo if he would be able to make wise laws for his people. The answer was, "The laws that you are about to make will be the best in the world." Of course he did not keep this a secret, and when he reached Sparta he found a large number of the people ready to agree with whatever he proposed. The baby king had become a man and held the throne, or, rather, held half of it, for it was the custom of the Spartans to have two kings. This plan does not seem to have been very successful, in this case at least, for one of them was too gentle and yielding to punish wrong-doing; and so the two never agreed, and their power was every day becoming less. They hoped that Lycurgus would strengthen it, and therefore they gave him a warm welcome. Then the whole little state watched to see what this wise man would do.

First of all, he had a senate of thirty members elected. These were chosen from among the older men, and were to remain senators as long as they lived. Five eph'ors, or overseers, were also chosen, and they held office for but one year. The real government was in their hands, for they could call even the kings to account if they thought it necessary; in important cases they acted as judges; and they decided whether there should be war or peace. The

Lycurgus's voluntary exile

SPARTAN FOOT
SOLDIER

kings were members of the senate, and in war times they commanded the army. They had little more power than the other senators, but they must have been far more comfortable than before the return of Lycurgus, for now they understood exactly what they could do, and knew that they would be supported in doing it.

Iron money

Lycurgus next set to work to divide the land equally among the citizens. They finally agreed to this; but when he proposed to divide the gold and silver in the same fashion, the wealthy folk said "No." They had a ruler, however, who knew how to get what he wanted in one way if he could not in another; and he simply decreed that gold and silver should no longer be counted as money, but that iron should be used instead. Little could be bought with this iron, for the far-sighted ruler had taken the temper out of it, so it was useless; and it was not a convenient sort of treasure to hoard up, for it was so cheap that fifteen hundred dollars' worth of it would fill a good-sized room.

Simple fare

The next aim of Lycurgus was to keep the Spartans from having dainties at table; and therefore he made them all, the kings as well as the other men, eat in public and fare alike. Even the hungriest could hardly have enjoyed the meals until he was well used to them, for the principal dish was a certain black broth that no one but Spartans seemed to find endurable. An Athenian who once tasted it declared that now he understood why Spartans were so fearless in war. "They would rather die than live on such fare as this," he said.

Plain houses

To keep the Spartans from furnishing their houses luxuriously, with golden cups, bright-colored coverlets, and bedsteads with silver feet, a law was made that the ceilings should be wrought with no tool but the axe, and the doors with none but the saw.

Lycurgus knew that the good taste of his countrymen would not permit them to bring costly furnishings into a house whose doors did not fit, and whose ceilings were nothing but rough logs. The story is told of a Spartan who in later years was a guest in a handsome house in Corinth, that he looked up at the ceilings, made of finely smoothed and carved planks, and asked with a little scorn, "Do the trees grow square in your country?"

So it was that Lycurgus made his countrymen live plainly and simply. That was well for the time being, he thought; but all these people had once been used to comfort, and he knew that when he died they would gradually slip back into their old luxurious fashions. Moreover, he wished to build up a nation that would not only do without luxuries, but would honestly despise them; and the only way to do this was to begin with the children. Then, when the boys and girls were grown up, Sparta would be full of men and women who had always lived simply and who scorned any other mode of life. There was little question that even a few thousand such men, taught to be soldiers, would be able to hold their own in battle against much larger numbers of the enemy. For these reasons he paid far more attention to the children than to the grown folk.

The children of Sparta

SPARTAN SOLDIER READY FOR THE ATTACK

"Children belong to the state," he declared, "and the state needs men and women who are strong and well." Therefore when a baby boy was born, a committee of wise men examined it to see if it was healthy. If it appeared weak or feeble, it was simply tossed into a cavern in the mountains to die. If the committee decided that it would probably grow into a strong man, it was given back to its father and mother. The boy was allowed to live with his parents only seven years; then each little fellow was made a member of a company of boys who lived under military rule. The one who seemed bravest was made captain, and the others had to obey whatever he commanded. Until the boys were twelve years old they ran about naked, so that they might become used to all kinds of weather. Even after that they were allowed to wear only one garment. For their beds they were sent to the river bank to break off reeds. When winter came, they were permitted, as a great luxury, to spread a little thistle-down over the reeds.

How Spartan boys were trained

At twelve the boys were put under the charge of a young man of twenty, called an i'ren, and were obliged to obey his orders. He would often send them for food or firewood; and they were expected to steal this as slyly as if they were in the country of an enemy. If they succeeded, they were praised; but if they were caught, they were severely whipped for their clumsiness. After supper the iren would often call the boys together and give them various tests. "Sing a song," he would command one boy. "Tell me who is the best man in the city," he would say to another; or, "What do you think of such and such an action?" The boys must not only answer the questions, but must give good reasons for their answers; and if they did not do well, they had to bear whatever punishment the iren might think they deserved. Of course the older men and the magistrates kept close watch of the iren, and after the younger boys had been sent away, he himself was soundly whipped if he had not ruled justly and wisely.

The girls were obliged to run and wrestle and throw quoits, but they were not treated nearly so severely as the boys. Indeed, whatever the boys did and wherever they went, some one was always on the watch to punish them if they did not do as well as was expected of them. One reason for these many whippings was that they might learn to despise pain. Once at least the older boys were brought before one of the altars and flogged, and the boy who bore the pain longest without an outcry received a prize. They became so proud of bearing pain well that sometimes one fell dead under this flogging without once having cried out or groaned. Why the boys were whipped

As to learning, the boys were taught music and poetry and a little reading, writing, and arithmetic; but much time was given to training them to talk. They were expected to be silent unless they had something to say; and when they did speak, they were required to use as few words as possible and to make their replies keen and pointed. Lycurgus himself practiced what he preached. The studies of Spartan boys

SHORT SWORDS OF THE SPARTANS

When an Athenian once made fun of the short swords of the Spartans, he retorted, "And yet we can reach our enemies' hearts with them." When he was asked whether he intended to build a wall around Sparta, he replied, "That city is well fortified which has a wall of men instead of brick." Some one asked a Spartan to come to hear a person who could imitate a nightingale. "I have heard the nightingale herself," was his reply. This brief, pointed manner of speaking took its name from that of the country, and has been called "laconic" from that day to this.

After twenty years of this training the Spartan was ready to begin to be a soldier; and he thought that any other occupation was beneath his dignity. Even the work of cultivating his own land he looked upon with the utmost scorn. That was the business of Helots, he declared.

The promise of the Spartans

One day, after Lycurgus had become an old man, he called the people together and said, "There is one thing more that is necessary to the happiness of the state. It is more important than all that has been done; but what it is I cannot tell you until I have come back from Delphi. Will you solemnly swear to obey the laws until I return?" They all took a solemn oath to be obedient, and he set out for Delphi with his son and some of his dearest friends. There he sacrificed to Apollo and asked, "Are the laws that I have made sufficient to promote virtue and secure the happiness of the state?" "They are excellent, and the city that keeps to them will be the most glorious in the world," was the response. Lycurgus wrote this oracle and sent it back to Sparta; but he himself did not return, for he had planned a way to make the Spartans keep his laws forever. He offered

LYCURGUS
(In the Museum at Naples)

up another sacrifice, and bade his son and friends farewell. After that, he refused all food and quietly waited for death. One last request he made. It was that after his body had been burned, the ashes should not be carried to Sparta but thrown into the sea. "Then, surely, no one can ever declare that I have returned," he said, "and the Spartans can never claim that they are released from their oath to keep my laws."

The death of Lycurgus

It seems more probable that these strange customs grew up little by little than that any one man had the power to oblige his fellow countrymen to change their whole manner of living. However that may be, and whether such a man as Lycurgus ever lived or not, these were the customs of the Spartans, and they really became a nation of soldiers. In Bœ-o'tia, a country a little north of Sparta, a poet named He'si-od was composing his "Works and Days," a poem about living quietly and peacefully in the country and doing whatever kind of work each season required; but the Spartans would have scorned such teachings. They were soldiers, and wartime was their holiday. When the enemy was near, the king sacrificed a goat, the men put garlands upon their heads, the musicians played a march, and the army moved forward joyfully. They knew how much better soldiers they were than other tribes, and they had little fear of being beaten.

Hesiod, eighth century B. C.

They looked upon war as a luxury, but it would seem as if they must have had as much as any one could want of fighting. Their first business was to make themselves so strong in Laconia that they would be free to win other lands. They succeeded in this, and then they began to think about Messenia, the country lying to the west of them. It was small wonder that they wanted it, for it was the most fertile country in the Peloponnesus, with hills and meadows, plenty of water, and excellent pasturage for cattle. After a good deal of fighting the Spartans got possession of Messenia. So much we may be sure of, but little is known about the war. There is a story, which may or may not be true, that at length matters looked so bad for the Messenians that they shut themselves up in I-tho'me and sent to Delphi to ask what to do. "The tribe that first places one hundred tripods on the altar of Zeus at Ithome will conquer," declared the oracle. Then the Messenians were jubilant, and they set to work to make one hun-

The first Messenian War, eighth century B. C.

Story of the tripods

dred wooden tripods. Unluckily for them, the Spartans, too, had learned of the response. "We will not wait to make tripods of wood," they said, "we will make them of clay." The result was that, while the Messenians were still working on their wooden tripods, a Spartan with a big bag on his shoulder contrived to slip into Ithome one afternoon. On the following morning the Messenians lost all hope, for there stood the Spartan tripods ranged about the altar. It was not long before Ithome fell; the Spartans had conquered. The Messenians were allowed to keep their land, but had to give half its produce to their conquerors. They had become the slaves of the Spartans.

AN ARMY LEADER

The story goes on to say that many years later, the grandsons of the warriors of Ithome determined to be ruled by Sparta no longer. They fought so fiercely that it was soon the turn of their enemies to beg Apollo for advice. "You must ask Athens to send you a leader," was the reply. This did not please the Spartans, but they made the request. The Athenians were not at all

The second Messenian War, seventh century B. C.

willing to help Sparta become stronger, but they did not dare disobey Apollo. Finally they made a plan which they thought exceedingly crafty. They sent for a leader a man named Tyrtæ'us, a schoolmaster who knew nothing about making war. They forgot, however, that Tyrtæus was also a poet; and while they were boasting of their cunning, he was making such ringing war-songs for the Spartans that they no longer remembered their discouragement, but marched cheerfully into battle, singing: —

"Now fight we for our children, for this land;
   Our lives unheeding, let us bravely die.
Courage, ye youths! together firmly stand;
   Think not of fear, nor ever turn to fly."

Finally the Spartans were successful; and now they ruled all the southern part of the Peloponnesus, from sea to sea.

The Spartans were in no hurry to give up fighting, and before many years had passed, they found an excuse for invading Ar-ca'di-a, the country lying north of Laconia. There is a legend that during the war the Messenians had hired some bands of Arcadian soldiers, and that after the war closed the Arcadians had allowed some of the Messenians to make homes for themselves in Arcadia. That was enough, and the Spartans set out with their weapons and wreaths and war-songs, and also some chains with which to bind the captives that they expected to take. The Spartans invade Arcadia

Arcadia was a quiet, pleasant country, with rugged mountains and swiftly flowing brooks in the north, and fresh green meadows in the south. The people who dwelt there kept flocks and herds. The Arcadian War They loved the music of the flute and they followed the old simple customs. They loved liberty, too, and they were hardy mountaineers; and, much to the surprise of the Spartans, it came to pass that some of them were bound with their own chains. The invaders won several victories, but they never really conquered the little mountainous country. Each army found what brave men there were on the other side, and the two peoples

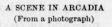

A SCENE IN ARCADIA
(From a photograph)

finally made a treaty by which they agreed to stand together in war. Sparta was to take the lead on the battlefield, but the Arcadians were always to hold the left wing, the place of honor.

The greatest honor, however, that could be held by any country of Greece was that of presiding at the Olympian games. Olympia was in the land of the Pi-sa'tans, and in the earliest days they were in charge. After a while the inhabitants of E'lis overcame the Pisatans in war, and then the E'li-ans proudly took the first position. Again and again the Pisatans revolted, and finally they found a powerful friend in Phei'don, the ruler of Ar'gos; for he was very willing to increase his power in the west. The Spartans, too, had no objection to increasing their power; they stood for the rights of Elis, and were victorious.

So it was that Sparta rose to power. By the middle of the sixth century before Christ, the Spartans ruled the southern part of the Peloponnesus; they had made an alliance with Arcadia; and were good friends with Elis. They had also succeeded in overthrowing the power of Argos, the state that had once been the mightiest in the Peninsula. The last battle took place at Thyr'e-a, which the Spartans captured; but the Ar'gives suffered a much more severe loss a few years later. They had fled from the Spartans to a sacred grove, and there their enemies surrounded them and set

the grove afire. Two thirds of their whole army perished. They still declared that Argos was a free city; but the Spartans cared little about that, so long as it had become too weak to interfere with them.

Such is the story of Sparta from the earliest times to the middle of the sixth century before Christ, — the story of a little wandering tribe who made their way into the country of their enemies and succeeded in becoming the most powerful people in the land.

SUMMARY

The Greeks loved their own land and were also fond of adventure. The Dorians came from the north and made the old inhabitants of the south into Periœki or Helots. They trained their whole tribe to be soldiers. Their story was that this was the work of a man named Lycurgus.

Lycurgus was said to have given the chief power of the government to five ephors, to have divided the land equally, to have used iron for money, to have obliged all to eat at the common table and to live in simple houses, and to have brought up the boys under military rule. He was said to have made the Spartans promise to keep his laws till his return; then to have gone away and taken his own life.

The Spartans made slaves of the Messenians, made a treaty with the Arcadians, and won the friendship of the Elians. They overthrew the power of Argos, and by the middle of the sixth century B. C. had become the strongest tribe in the land.

SUGGESTIONS FOR WRITTEN WORK

Why would a Greek wish to stay in his own country?
Some one tells the Dorians about the country lying to the south.
A Spartan boy tells another boy about his life.
A visit to Arcadia.

V

THE EARLY DAYS OF ATHENS: THE LAWS OF SOLON

SPARTA was the chief state of the Peloponnesus, and even north of the Peloponnesus she began to be looked upon as the leading state of Greece. Her great rival was Attica. Attica was a penin- Attica sula about eighty miles long, bounded by mountains on the north and west. There were a few rivers, but even the largest had a way of running dry in warm weather. The soil was scanty and barren. A Greek could make a good meal of a piece of bread, a cup of wine, and a handful of olives; but even these could not be obtained in Attica nearly so easily as in the neighboring state, Bœotia, for to produce them, the ground had to be cultivated with great care. There was one advantage, however, that made up for these disadvantages, and that was the fine climate. Attica was warmer in the winter and cooler in the summer than

VIEW OF REGION AROUND ATHENS
(From a photograph)

Bœotia. The air was so pure that distant objects could be seen far more distinctly than elsewhere. The heavens were so bright and clear that it was a pleasure to gaze up into them; and even if the mountains were somewhat barren, the sunset skies were so glowing that the delicate outlines of the peaks traced upon them were wonderfully beautiful. The people were Ionians. They said proudly, "No foreign conquerors have ever overcome us. We are sprung from the soil itself." This is why the Athenian women liked to wear ornaments in the form of a cicada, — because it was believed that the cicada was born of the earth.

Not much was known of Attica in the earliest times; but as there were no Greek slaves in the state, the belief was probably true that it had never been conquered by foreigners, but had

been formed by a union of people of the same race. The Greeks
believed that this union had been brought about by the hero
Theseus, who was once their king; and there were stories without
number of his exploits. He was declared not only to have killed Theseus in
Attica
the Minotaur, but to have gone on a warlike expedition with
Heracles, and to have sailed in the Argo in quest of the Golden
Fleece. It is said that as a young man he dressed so foppishly,
with his elegant robes, his jewels, and his perfumes, that one day
as he was passing some workmen they first stared, then laughed
and said, "That young girl is old enough to be married; how happens it that she is running about the streets alone?" Theseus
heard this speech, and to show that he was something more than
a dandy, he stopped a cart that was going by, unyoked the oxen,
and tossed them over a temple.
When he came to be king, the
stories say that he invited not
only people dwelling in Attica, but even strangers, to
make homes for themselves in
Athens. The city was then
only a cluster of little houses
on a great mass of rock with
a wide, flat top; but it was a
very safe place, for it would

THE THESEUM AS IT IS TO-DAY
(A temple in Athens where, according to the legend,
the remains of Theseus were buried)

not be easy for enemies to make their way up the rock and into
the city. Theseus was not greedy of power, for when the inhab- Beginning of
itants of the other parts of Attica hesitated to agree to be ruled Athens
by a court in Athens, he said to them, "If you will do this, I will
give up my rights. You shall be king as much as I, save that
I shall watch over the laws, and if there is a war, I shall com-

mand the army." It is no wonder that they yielded to so generous a prince. Theseus set up a pillar to show just where the limits of Attica began. Then he established splendid festivals in honor of the union of the Attic villages.

Codrus

The next great king, according to the legends, was Co'drus. He had reigned peacefully for some time when trouble came upon him. The Spartans and some other Dorians united to attack Athens, and encamped before the walls of the city. They were in the best of spirits, for the oracle had said, "If you spare the life of Codrus, you will be sure of victory." Of course they would spare the life of Codrus, — that was a small price to pay for victory, — and soon Athens would be theirs. If they had known what sort of man King Codrus was, they would not have been quite so jubilant. A friend of his who lived at Delphi told him what the oracle had said; and in a moment the brave king had made up his mind what to do. He dressed himself like a wood-chopper, slipped out of the city gates, and went where he was sure to meet some of the Dorians. Soon he came upon two of them. He struck one with his axe and killed him. Then the other one killed Codrus. By this time the Athenians

His patriotism

had learned that their king had died for them, and they sent out a messenger to beg for his body. The Dorians were terrified when they learned what they had done. "It is of no use to attack Athens," they said, "for the gods will be against us"; and so they turned about and marched over the Isthmus of Corinth and back to the Peloponnesus, and Athens was saved. The Athenians were so grateful that they declared their city should never have another king, that the title should always remain sacred to the patriot Codrus.

There were later kings, nevertheless, but they had to share

their authority with eight other men called ar'chons, or rulers, until at last the king-archon did little more than offer up the state sacrifices to the gods. All the nine archons together had not nearly so much power as a famous council, called the A-re-op'a-gus be-cause it met on the Hill of Mars, or Ares, which made all the laws and tried men accused of crime.

MARS HILL, WHERE THE AREOPAGUS HELD ITS SESSIONS

This seems like a good plan for a government, but there was one thing that made it extremely unfair, namely, that all these archons and councilors were nobles, or Eu'pat-rids, that is, men of high birth. They were generally wealthy, and they made laws which were convenient and comfortable for the rich, but which bore hard upon the poor. The government, then, was an oligarchy, or rule of the few; and an oligarchy is seldom fair to all the people. Some of the poorer men of Attica lived on the estates of the Eupatrids, and if they did not pay their rent, the owners of the estates had the right to sell them and their families as slaves. Even those who had little farms of their own were not much better off, for many of them had been obliged to borrow money of the nobles, which they had little hope of paying. Therefore, on many of the farms a pillar was set up on which was cut the amount that the farmer owed and the name of the man to whom the farm was mortgaged. Sometimes the poor farmers became so discouraged that they sold their children as slaves to try to pay even the interest on these harassing mortgages. The Eupatrids enjoyed themselves, but it is no wonder that the poorer people became more and more miserable. Some went away as colonists, and those who remained were greatly dissatisfied.

At last even the comfortable Eupatrids saw that something **The laws of** must be done to quiet the troubles. One thing that the people **Draco** found especially unjust was that the laws had never been published, and if a Eupatrid took away their property, they had no way of knowing whether he was acting lawfully or unlawfully. "If we publish the laws, they will be satisfied," thought the nobles; and they chose a Eupatrid named Dra'co to put together what they had generally agreed to call the laws, and revise them. Long after the time of Draco, the laws had become so much milder that people said his had been "written in blood," but they were really more reasonable than the unwritten laws that had been in force before his day. Moreover, his code gave far greater **"The** power to the people who were not nobles, " the Many," as the **Many"** Eupatrids called them; for it declared that the magistrates need not be Eupatrids, but might be chosen from the members of the Ec-cle'si-a, or general assembly, who received a certain income from land. The code even allowed the Ecclesia to choose them. This was a great gain to "the Many," for every man who was able to provide himself with weapons for battle had a right to belong to the Ecclesia.

The Council   Draco also formed from the whole body of citizens a Council, part of whose business it was to propose laws to the Ecclesia.

This code of Draco's was excellent in some ways; but he forgot one important fact, namely, that people who were poor and hungry and were in danger of being sold as slaves would not feel much more contented because some men a little better off than

THE ACROPOLIS AT ATHENS
(As it appeared at the height of Athens's glory)

they had now the right to vote for a magistrate. One of the
Eupatrids named Cy'lon thought this was a good time to try to
make himself tyrant. He and his followers took possession of the
great rock, the A-crop'o-lis, expecting that "the Many" would
join them. This did not come to pass, and soon they were surrounded by the war-archon Meg'a-cles and the troops of the state.
Cylon escaped, and his followers ran into the temple of Athene
which stood on the Acropolis. Then Megacles was in a dilemma.
It would be a crime against the goddess to attack even rebels
when they had fled to her for protection; and it would pollute the
temple if men were left to starve and die in it. At last he sent a
message to the rebels: "If you will yield, I will spare your lives."

The revolt of Cylon

The rebels agreed, but they did not feel quite sure that the archon would keep his word; so when they left the temple they tied a cord to Athene's shrine, and came down from the Acropolis holding it fast. Probably they held it a little too fast, for suddenly it

A BUST IN THE MUSEUM OF NA-
PLES, THOUGHT TO BE THAT OF
SOLON

broke. "The goddess refuses to protect you," cried Megacles, and fell upon the defeated men. Some were cut into pieces and some stoned to death. Then it was the turn of the Athenians to be frightened. "Athene will surely punish our city," they wailed; and they demanded that Megacles should be banished. Some of the nobles agreed with them, but others were not willing to give up a fellow noble. At length, by the influence of a wise Eupatrid named So'lon, Megacles was tried. The result was that he and his whole clan, the Alc-mæ-on'i-dæ, were banished.

Solon was by no means a stranger to his countrymen. It was because of him that the island of Sal'a-mis now belonged to Attica. Both Athens and the city of Meg'a-ra had claimed it, and when their dispute came to war, the Athenians were so badly beaten and so hopeless that they made a law saying, "Whoever proposes to renew the war against Megara shall be put to death." Solon felt that it was a disgrace to his country to give up Salamis, but he had no wish to be put to death. At length he made a plan to arouse his countrymen. He shut himself up in his own house and let the story go abroad that he was insane. In reality,

he was composing a stirring poem about Salamis. One day he
suddenly ran into the market-place, where there was always a
crowd ready to listen to anything new, and recited his poem.
It began,

> " Hear and attend: from Salamis I came
> To show your error."

A madman could not be punished for breaking a law, and the
Athenians were so aroused by this poem that they determined
to renew the war. They seem to have decided that Solon was
insane enough not to be punished, but quite sane enough to be
a good general; so they put him in command of their forces.
Salamis finally fell into the hands of the Athenians.

For these reasons, both the Eupatrids and "the Many" felt a
good deal of confidence in Solon, and gave him the right to do
whatever he thought would improve matters. There was certainly need of some man
of wisdom, for all Attica
was in an uproar. Besides
the troubles between the
poor and the rich, there
were also three parties
who were always quarrel-
ing: the men of the plains,
who lived on the most fertile land; the men of the

FARMER GOING TO MARKET

coast, who lived near the sea and were fishers and traders; and
the men of the mountains, or shepherds, who lived on the rugged
hillsides where they pastured their flocks.

These people had different wishes; and no man, however wise
he might be, could ever have pleased them all. Solon paid little

attention to what any one class of people wanted, but did just what he thought would be best for the whole state. The most pressing trouble was that so many people were in debt. The farmers were rapidly losing their farms and becoming day-laborers, while the laborers were being sold as slaves. So many had been sold, that their absence was a great loss to the country.

The decrees of Solon

Solon's first decrees were that men might pay their debts in new coins only three fourths as heavy as the old ones, but counted as of the same value; that the debts of farmers who had borrowed of the state should be forgiven; that a man who had agreed to become the slave of another if he did not return borrowed money, should not be held to his bargain; that all who had already become slaves should be freed; and that those who had been sold into foreign lands should be brought back at the expense either of the state or of the man who had sold them.

At the first glance these laws seem rather unfair to the creditors; but as a general thing, when a rich man lent money to a poor man, he knew perfectly well that he could never be repaid; his object was to get the man himself, that is, to make free citizens into slaves, and no law ought to protect such dealings.

Other reforms

Solon himself was a Eupatrid, but he did not believe that the Eupatrids alone ought to make the laws. He divided the people into four classes according to their income from land. The rich held more offices, but they had to pay larger taxes. The members of the lowest class, those who were too poor to buy arms and armor for themselves, could not be elected to any office, but they paid no tax; and every man, rich or poor, belonged to the Ecclesia and had the right to vote. So it was that Solon lived up to his favorite saying, "Equality causes no war." With these new laws, every man had the opportunity to rise from one class to another, and finally to hold the highest office in the state. He might even become a member of the Areopagus, and in the eyes of an Athenian this was the noblest of civic honors. Most of the laws of Draco were abolished, and Solon made a new code. Finally, he pardoned the Alcmæonidæ and allowed them to return to Athens. He did not decree how children should be brought up, but he evidently meant that they should not be idle, for he declared that no man should be required to support his father in old age unless the father had taught him as a boy to support himself by some trade. Solon's whole thought was the good of the state. He did not, like Lycurgus, believe in despising money, but rather in using it so carefully and wisely that when it was needed there

Laws of Draco abolished

PREPARING FOR THE FUNERAL
(From a vase painting)

would be no lack. For this reason he made some laws limiting the amount that might be spent at funerals, where there had usually been much display, and also some about the dress of women; for instance, when a woman went on a journey, she might carry with her only three dresses. The laws were written on wooden tablets, and these were set up where every one could read them.

Laws against extravagance

There were so many different parties in Athens that no one of them was perfectly satisfied. They came to Solon again and again. "What does this law mean?" they would ask, or "Why not change that law?" At length Solon decided that he would go away and leave the people and the laws together for a while. When he returned to Athens, however, he found that the citizens were no more contented than when he left them. The nobles had supposed that all would be peaceful after the debts were forgiven, and they felt as if their losses had gone for nothing. Many of the poor people were grievously disappointed, for they had expected that in some mysterious way their friend Solon would make them all rich. The nobles did not agree among themselves, and the three parties, the men of the plains, of the coast, and of the mountains, were still at odds.

SUMMARY

Attica was not generally fertile, but had a fine climate.

The Athenians believed that Theseus had formed the state by uniting many Ionians.

Codrus gave his life for Athens.

Later, the state was ruled by the king and eight archons, subject to the Areopagus.

The government was an oligarchy, and the laws favored the rich. Draco revised them. His code allowed the Ecclesia to choose magistrates from among all citizens who owned a certain amount of land.

Cylon attempted to become tyrant, Megacles overcame him, but in so doing violated the shrine of Athene. For this crime he and the other Alcmæonidæ were banished.

There were not only troubles between the rich and the poor, but there were three parties, the men of the plains, of the coast, and of the mountains.

Solon made laws to favor the poor. He divided the people into

four classes, according to their property. He allowed the Alcmæonidæ to return. He obliged the people to be economical. No one
was fully satisfied with these laws.

SUGGESTIONS FOR WRITTEN WORK

What would one have seen in passing through Attica?
A poor man of Attica tells his troubles.
One of Cylon's followers describes the action of Megacles.

VI

THE RULE OF PISISTRATUS AND THE ALCMÆONIDÆ

THE Athenians were aggrieved and restless and ready to welcome almost any change. This was just the time for a crafty
man to step in, win favor, and become tyrant. There was a man
ready to do this. His name was Pi-sis′tra-tus. He was popular
because of his generosity and because of his having won victories in the Olympian chariot-races. He pretended to be perfectly
satisfied with Solon's laws and to care for nothing but the good
of his country. The people believed him, and when he drove
into the market-place one day smeared with blood, they were
ready to accept his story that his enemies had almost killed him
because he was so devoted to the happiness of the people. The
market-place was full of the poorest men, the ones to whom
Pisistratus claimed to be a special friend. Solon, too, was there,
and he cried out, "Pisistratus, you have done this to impose
upon your countrymen." Nevertheless, the people believed the
deceiver and were ready to fall in with a proposal — made by a

Pisistratus becomes tyrant, sixth century B.C

man whom he had engaged beforehand — that their **abused** friend should have a bodyguard of fifty men, armed with clubs. Little by little the number was increased. "The Many" wished it, and the nobles did not dare to oppose them too strongly. After a while the guard had come to consist of four hundred strong

THE ACROPOLIS AT ATHENS
(As it appears to-day)

men. Then Pisistratus seized the Acropolis. He became tyrant, and Athens was no longer free. Solon had warned the Athenians again and again, but they had not heeded him. At last he laid his shield and sword down outside his door and closed it, saying, "I have done all in my power to defend my country and its laws."

Pisistratus now felt himself master of Athens. "How will he treat Solon?" the people questioned. They soon learned that he had no idea of doing him any harm. On the contrary, he often asked his advice in public matters; and Solon was generous and patriotic enough never to refuse it if he thought it would be of benefit to the state.

Pisistratus banished the Alcmæonidæ, but in a little while he himself was driven away. He succeeded in returning, and a wonderful return it was. It took place on a festival day, when the streets were full of people watching the processions in honor of the gods. One procession after another had passed, when suddenly the loud voices of heralds were heard crying, "Ye men of Athens, receive and welcome Pisistratus! Athene honors him

above all other men, and now brings him back into her own His return
Acropolis!" A brilliant escort followed, and then a splendid

GREEK CHARIOTS *Flaxman*

chariot rolled along, wherein sat a tall, handsome woman dressed in a full suit of armor with shield and spear, and looking much as the Greeks fancied Athene to look.

Beside the chariot rode the tyrant. The people gazed and gazed. "It is the goddess herself!" some of them whispered in awe; others saw that it was only a trick; but the gates of the Acropolis were thrown open, and Pisistratus was again tyrant of Athens. Once more he was driven from the city, and this time he returned by force of arms. At last he was secure in his position, and he held it until his death eighteen years later.

Of course the rule did not rightfully belong to Pisistratus, but no one could deny that he made good use of it. It is true that he kept the highest offices for members of his own clan, but he was kind to the poor farmers and gave them cattle and seeds and farming tools. He beautified the city with mag-

The rule of Pisistratus

ATHENE
(In the Vatican Gallery at Rome)

Improvements made

nificent temples; he built a massive aqueduct to bring down water from the mountains; and he laid out a delightful garden on the bank of a river near the city. Here were stately buildings and fountains and pleasant walks in shady groves. Here it was that the young men of Athens used to come for military exercises.

HERMES POST
(In the Louvre)

He built roads to different parts of the country. They all started from an altar in Athens, and there tablets were kept on which the distances to the various places were written. The roads themselves were made much more agreeable for travelers, for milestones were put up, not plain stones, but wooden posts whose tops were carved into heads of Hermes, the god to whom men who were about to go on a journey prayed for protection. Often some amusing saying was cut on the post. Of course Pisistratus did not forget Athene. There is an old story that she and Poseidon once vied with each other to see which could bestow the more valuable gift upon the city. Poseidon gave a spring of salt water, and Athene gave an olive tree. It was decided that her gift was the more valuable. Her name was given to the city, and she was always held in the highest reverence. Pisistratus built a temple for

Athene honored

her worship, and every year he held a brilliant festival in her honor. The early Greeks believed that the image of a goddess was in some degree the goddess herself, and they felt sure that Athene was delighted when at this festival they formed an imposing procession and carried to the temple a dazzling new robe to put upon her statue. All those things vanished long ago, and, however much they may have pleased the Athenians, they make little difference to us. Pisistratus is said to have done one deed, however, for which we may feel grateful, even after twenty-four

hundred years have passed; he is said to have asked all the
people who knew the works of Homer and of Hesiod to meet
together in Athens and
compare the poems as
they had been used to
recite them. The ver-
sion that was decided
to be best was care-
fully put into writing;
and this is how it came
about that we can read
the thoughts of those
two great writers in

HORSEMEN HASTENING TO JOIN THE PROCESSION
TO THE TEMPLE OF ATHENE
(From the Parthenon frieze)

almost the same words in which the early Greeks read them.
Pisistratus was not satisfied with doing honor to dead poets; he
invited the best of the poets then living to make their homes
in Athens, and he saw
to it that they should
live in comfort.

When Pisistratus
died, in 527 B. C., no
one tried to prevent
his son Hip'pi-as from
succeeding him. At
first, Hippias was kind
to the people, but
after a while he and

HORSEMEN IN THE PROCESSION
(From the Parthenon frieze)

his younger brother Hip-par'chus became so haughty and insolent that a plot was made to assassinate them. Hippias escaped,
but his brother was slain. After this Hippias showed himself so

tyrannical that those who had once liked him began to wish for his downfall. There were also some people away from Athens who wished the same thing. These were the Alcmæonidæ, who had been in exile all this time. They had always hoped to return, and they were wise enough to know that the first step was to win the favor of the priests at Delphi. They watched for an opportunity, and at length it came. The temple of Apollo at Delphi

The Alcmæonidæ rebuild the temple of Apollo

caught fire and burned. "We will rebuild it for three hundred talents," said the Alcmæonidæ; and the bargain was made. Now was their chance. They not only kept the bargain, but they did much more, for they made the statues and carvings, indeed the whole building, far more handsome in every way than they had agreed. They had promised, for instance, to make the porch of the temple of limestone; but instead of ordinary limestone, they used the purest and whitest of Pa'ri-an marble.

HEAD OF APOLLO BELVEDERE
(In the Vatican Gallery at Rome)

The Greeks were delighted, and the priests of Apollo were ready to do anything for the generous Alcmæonidæ. It was an easy matter for them to do favors so long as they had control of the oracle,

The return of the Alcmæonidæ

and they set to work to bring the Alcmæonidæ back to Athens. The Spartans were good fighters, and they had long wished to make Attica subject to them; so now, whenever they asked the oracle for advice about any undertaking, the answer was always,

"First set Athens free." At length, the Spartan king Cle-om'e-nes marched out with his army, and before long the Alcmæonidæ had come back to Athens, and Hippias had been obliged to go into exile.

The leader of the Alcmæonidæ was Clis'the-nes, and he soon became ruler. He succeeded in bringing about two changes that were exceedingly good for his country: he made the people more united, and he gave the common folk a larger share in the government. He set about uniting the people by dividing them in quite a different fashion from the way in which they had been divided before. There had been four "I-on'ic Tribes," as they were called, and every man looked up to the great folk of his own tribe and belonged to some party. Clisthenes determined to break up these parties, and this is the way he did it. He divided the whole country into districts called demes. Then he made a tribe, consisting of the people of one deme in the north of Attica, another in the south, and so on. There were ten of these tribes, but the men of the different demes were strangers to one another; and so it was not now nearly so easy as it had been for a discontented noble to raise a party to support him. Since the days of Draco there had been a Council which proposed laws to the people, and Clisthenes now gave each tribe the right to elect fifty members. However, each tribe chose a governor for itself, and also a general, who commanded the army in turn with the other nine, one day at a time. No change was made, however, in the division of the citizens into four classes according to their income from land, and it was still impossible for a man in the fourth class to hold office.

The government of Attica was now a democracy, or government by the people. In the earlier times no one could be a magis-

The reforms of Clisthenes

Attica divided into ten tribes

Attica
becomes a
democracy

trate who was not a Eupatrid. Draco allowed the Ecclesia to choose the magistrates from among those who received a certain income from land. He admitted all to the Ecclesia who could buy arms and armor for themselves. Solon allowed no one to be chosen as magistrate unless, as in Draco's day, he received a certain income from land;

SACRIFICE TO ATHENE, THE GODDESS OF ATHENS
(The priestess with the branches is sprinkling the altar.
The priest stands at the right)

but he admitted all to the Ecclesia, whether they could buy arms for themselves or not. Clisthenes did not allow the men of the fourth class to hold office, but he gave the people as a whole much more power than they had previously had. There were many new citizens, for Clisthenes allowed men who had come to Attica from other countries, and even those who had once been slaves, to become citizens.

In order to give still more power to the people, and make it impossible for any man to become tyrant, Clisthenes introduced two remarkable customs. One was called ostracism. If the Council and the general assembly of the people thought that any man was getting so much power that he might become tyrant, they asked the citizens to come together. Then each one was requested to write on a shell (ostrakon) or bit of pottery the name of any man whom he believed about to become dangerous to the liberty of the state. If any one man received six thousand votes, he must leave Athens for ten years. This

Ostracism

banishment was not agreeable, of course, but it was looked upon as a sort of compliment, for it was really saying to a man, "You are greater or more popular than any other person in the state."

The second custom was intended to prevent wealthy or powerful men from raising parties to elect them to office. If a man wished to hold some office, all that he could do now was to present his name as a candidate. Then lots were drawn to decide who should be the successful man. Of course the Greeks were not so foolish as to choose their generals in this manner; and, whatever the faults of the two customs were, they did at least keep Athens free from tyrants. *Election by lot*

The common people were pleased with these changes, but the nobles were not, and they began to make plans to break up the democracy. They appealed to the Spartan ruler for help. King Cleomenes knew that if Athens were a democracy and the masses of the people were contented, there would be little hope of his gaining power in Attica. Moreover, he felt that he had been only a cat's-paw in bringing back the Alcmæonidæ, and had gained nothing for Sparta. Therefore, he was not only willing to help, but he induced some of the allies of the Spartans to join him. The allies, however, withdrew, the Spartan leaders quarreled, and the whole army broke up. The people of Thebes and of Chal'cis had taken this time to march out against the Athenians. But the Athenians also marched out, and beat first the Thebans and then the Chal-cid'i-ans. Later the Spartans made an attempt to bring back Hippias, but the Athenians would not have him; and they were obliged to give up for the time the attempt to rule Attica. *The attempt of the Spartans to break up the democracy at Athens*

Athens had gained statues, buildings, wise laws, and a better government; but, best of all, she had reached the point where the masses of her citizens were united in caring for their country.

GOLD COIN OF ATHENS

(On one side is the head of Athene, with
helmet and crown of olive leaves; on
the reverse are two owls separated by
an olive branch)

SUMMARY

Pisistratus became tyrant of Athens. He banished the Alcmæonidæ, and was banished himself, but succeeded in returning. He was kind to the poor and beautified the city. He had the works of Homer and of Hesiod put into written form.

Pisistratus was succeeded by Hippias. The Alcmæonidæ rebuilt the temple of Apollo at Delphi, and the Spartans by command of the oracle brought them back to Athens and drove Hippias into exile.

Clisthenes became ruler of Athens. He made the people more united, and established a democracy. He introduced ostracism and election by lot.

SUGGESTIONS FOR WRITTEN WORK

A boy describes Pisistratus's coming into the market-place.

A poor man tells of the changes in government made by Clisthenes.

A man who had been ostracized describes the custom.

VII

THE OLYMPIAN GAMES

THERE was one thing in which the Greeks were united, and that was the games, already referred to, in which no one who was not a Greek could take part. The most famous were held at Olympia in Elis. Through all the changes in the different states these had been continued, and they were regarded as being so sacred that, no matter how fiercely two Greek tribes might be fighting, they always had a truce during the

A VIEW OF OLYMPIA
(The modern building is a museum containing many art treasures found at Olympia)

The truce of the games

time of the Olympian games and the days allowed for going and returning. No Greek who could afford to make the journey would think of losing a celebration of the games; and the roads leading to Olympia must have been a wonderfully interesting sight for a week or two before and after the midsummer days on which the festival was held.

Imagine the first day of the celebration! The different states had all sent representatives, and these men wore their richest garments and rode in the handsomest chariots that could be obtained. The Greeks enjoyed processions so much that there can

The first day

hardly fail to have been a parade of these, and after it there was almost certainly a solemn sacrifice to Zeus. Then came the important work of making sure that those who wished to engage in the games had a right to do so. Not only the athletes, but the umpires and trainers, had to swear that they were free-born Greeks of unmixed blood, and that they would obey the rules of the games. Even with this oath, they had also to prove their citizenship, and the athletes had to show that they had followed the rules of diet and training required. All this would occupy one day from morning till night. The following days — three and perhaps more — were given to the contests. There were racing, wrestling, boxing, leaping, throwing of quoits, and hurling of javelins. Last of all were the famous races of four-horse chariots. When the moment had come,

The celebration

The four-horse chariot race

THE WRESTLERS
(From a statue in the Uffizi Gallery at Florence)

there was a loud blast on the trumpets, the barriers fell, and the horses darted forward, while the crowd shouted and cheered in the wildest excitement.

The fifth day was given up to the victors. A boy was sent to the sacred grove to cut with a golden knife branches from a wild olive tree. These were made into wreaths, which were presented to the successful men. It was the proudest moment of a man's life when the herald called his name, his father's name, and that of his native city, and he stepped forward to receive his crown. The crowds shouted their applause, and he forgot the long, weary months of training and thought only of the fame that he had won.

YOUTH VICTORIOUS IN A HORSE-RACE

(The victor on the horse is preceded by the herald, who calls the name of the victor. In the rear is the man bearing on his head a tripod, the prize, and in his hand a wreath)

The olive wreath with all that it stood for was reward enough, but there were many more honors awaiting its happy wearer. He usually made a sacrifice to Zeus, and in this all his countrymen who were present were glad to join, for he had brought glory to their country. While the sacrifice was burning, they marched around the altar in a splendid procession, singing choruses of praise to the gods to the music of the flute and the cithara. This was only the beginning, for the sacrifice was followed by numerous banquets. The city that presided at the games gave feasts to the victors, and the victors gave feasts to their friends. Even this was not all, for often a statue in honor of the successful man was set up at Olympia, and maybe another at his own home. Even the return of a victor to his native city was a splendid sight. He was dressed

RUINS OF ENTRANCE TO THE FOOT-RACE COURSE AT OLYMPIA

(From a photograph)

in a rich purple robe, and brought to his home in a chariot drawn by four white horses. His friends and relatives followed him, all in their holiday garments; and then came a crowd, singing and cheering and shouting at the top of their voices. When they had come to the walls, the procession stopped. "What need of walls of defense for a city that has such men as he?" the people cried; and then a piece of the city wall was torn down and the four white horses pranced over the ruins. Of course banquets followed, and often a generous gift of gold and silver. The philosophers of the day sometimes reminded the citizens that these victors in the games were of small value to the state. "They are of no use in peace," declared the wise men, "for not

His triumphant home coming

THE TWO-HUNDRED YARD DASH

their minds but their bodies have been trained; and they are of no use in war, for their training is so one-sided that they soon break down if they attempt military service." Nevertheless, the worship of the athlete continued. In some places he dined every day at the expense of the city, and all the rest of his life had a front seat reserved for him in the theatre. His name was carefully inscribed on the register that was kept at Olympia, and he was honored as long as he lived.

The Olympiads

The Greeks had so much regard for these games that they dated events from them, counting the year of a celebration and the following three years as an "O-lym′pi-ad." For instance, 776 B. C. they called the first year of the first Olympiad; 770 B. C., the third year of the second Olympiad.

For more than a thousand years these games were continued

without a break. Their influence upon Greek life can hardly be rated too highly. They affected commerce, for where so many thousand people were gathered together, there must have been a vast amount of buying and selling. They affected art, for at the games the sculptor could find the finest of living models. They affected the manners of the people, their regard for religious rites, and also their interest in literature and oratory; for at most of the games contests in these lines also were held. The Greeks never became united into one nation, but the games did much to make them feel that they had interests in common, and that if a tribe called in the aid of a foreigner against another tribe, it was in some degree a traitor to the country.

Knille

THE OLYMPIA FOOT-RACE

SUMMARY

During the time of the Olympian games a truce was always held. No one not of pure Greek blood was allowed to contend. There were many kinds of contests. The victor was crowned with an olive wreath. There were sacrifices and banquets in his honor, and often statues of him were erected.

His return to his home was a splendid sight.

The philosophers claimed that the victors were of small value to the state, but the highest honors continued to be shown them.

The Greeks dated events from the games, counting every four years as an Olympiad.

The games affected commerce, art, manners, regard for religious rites, and interest in literature and oratory. They made the Greeks feel that they had something in common.

SUGGESTIONS FOR WRITTEN WORK

A boy describes a day at the games.

A victor writes a letter home telling of his triumph.

Why did the games affect the manners of the Greeks?

VIII

THE GREEK COLONIES: THE TYRANTS

The games did much to unite the Greeks and bind them to their fatherland, but, nevertheless, large numbers of them had left their homes and gone to other countries. There were three rea-sons for this emigration. One was that the cities were growing; many persons who had become wealthy had little share in the government, and they were dissatisfied and restless. A second

Why the Greeks founded colonies

reason was that those who were not rich were becoming more and more eager to make their fortunes as soon as possible. There were better opportunities to do this in the less settled lands than in Greece itself. Third, the Greeks liked adventure, and therefore a company could always be found ready to go to the eastward or even to sail away to see what might be discovered in the wonderland of the far west, that is, in Italy or Sicily or Sar-din'i-a. They could land and establish a colony almost

THE DELPHIC APOLLO

(From a vase-painting. The wings of the tripod were supposed to enable Apollo to fly over the sea to visit the colonies)

wherever they chose, for few of the tribes living along the coast of the Med-i-ter-ra'ne-an valued the shore or the harbors. Indeed, they were often glad to have the strangers come to their lands to trade with them. So it came about that between 750 B. C. and 600 B. C. Greek colonies were founded by the score. Men who wished to mine for silver and gold, went to Macedonia. Those who meant to buy fish or cattle or grain or slaves, sailed to the shores of the Eux'ine, or Black Sea. Those who expected to get rich by trading in amber and tin, journeyed to the coast of what is now called France; for those valuable articles could easily be brought from the north down the river Rhone. In earlier times settlements had been made on the islands and shores of the Ægean Sea, and now on the islands to the west of Greece, on the shores of Africa, in the Delta of the Nile, — wherever a company of

Greeks thought there was a good chance for trade, there Greek colonies were established.

Apollo was the god of colonizing, and of course no colonists **The value of** would set out before asking the advice of the oracle at Delphi. **the oracles** This advice was exceedingly valuable, for people from far and **to the** near came to consult the oracle, and the priests had much better **colonists** opportunities to learn about the different countries than other men. When a band of Greeks who wished to found a colony asked the oracle about the place to which they meant to go, they would perhaps learn that the land was not fertile, or that the natives were savage and warlike, or that there were no good

SAPPHO
(In the Louvre)

Pradier

harbors on that coast. Then the colonists would change their plans and choose some other place for their settlement.

Generally the colonists of **Life in** any one company came from **the colonies** the same city. They always carried with them some embers from the sacred fires of their home town, and with these they kindled the altar fires of their new home. They were not governed by the old city, however, but were free to rule themselves as they thought best. The colonies were not crowded: there was room for people to live in their own way. The thoughts of the colonists were more original and more bold; and for a long while the poets and philosophers of the colonies and the islands were greater than those of the mainland of Greece. The little island of Les'bos was the home of the poet Al-cæ'us and the poetess Sap'pho (Săf'fō). Alcæus wrote chiefly on political subjects, but he found time to compose a poem to Sappho, in which he called her "violet-weaving, pure, sweet-smiling Sappho." Sappho herself wrote such beautiful poems that people spoke of her, not as *a* poetess, but as *the* poetess. One pretty fancy of hers was: —

Alcæus, seventh century B. C.

Sappho, seventh century B. C.

> "The stars around the lovely moon
> Fade back and vanish very soon,
> When, round and full, her silver face
> Swims into sight, and lights all space."

The greatest philosopher of the time, Py-thag'o-ras, was also born on one of the Greek islands, Sa'mos, a bit of land only twenty-seven miles long. "What is a philosopher?" he was once asked by a king; and he replied: "At the games some try to win glory, some buy and sell for money, and some watch what the others do. So it is in life; and philosophers are those who watch, who study nature, and search for wisdom." There are many absurd stories about Pythagoras. One is that he tamed a savage bear by speaking to it; another that, as he was crossing a river, the stream cried out, "Hail, Pythagoras!" Even though he did not tame bears with a word or listen to the greetings of rivers, the stories show what a remarkable man people thought him. He was a deep thinker and very learned in mathematics. Some of his teachings, however, were most fanciful; for instance, he thought that, as the planets rolled on in their courses, they made a delightful harmony. "Why, then, do we not hear it?" questioned his disciples. "Because the music is too delicate for the ears of men," was his reply. One of his wise sayings was,

Pythagoras, sixth century B. C.

His teachings

SCHOOL OF PYTHAGORAS

Coomans

"Stir not a fire with a sword"; that is, If any one is angry, do not add to his wrath. Another was, "Leave not your post without the command of the general"; that is, Do not take your own life.

This colonizing went on, as has been said, between 750 B. C. and 600 B. C. During nearly those same years, most of the Greek states were changing their government. In the early days they had all been ruled by kings. The power of the kings grew less and less, and at length in nearly every country a few of the **The oligarchies** strongest families, owners of large estates, took the rule into their own hands. The government then became an oligarchy, that is, government by the few. These "few" claimed to be descendants of the heroes, and to be far greater and wiser than the common folk around them. The common folk did not always agree with them, and in most states some leader arose after a while who became ruler. Such a ruler was called a tyrant, that is, one whose power is above the laws.

In one way the rule of the tyrants was good for the states, for to win the favor of the gods they built many handsome **The tyrants** temples. The building of these and other public works made the cities far more beautiful than when the kings were in power, and also provided work for the people. Some of the tyrants were more kind than the kings had been; nevertheless, the Greeks did not like the idea of being ruled without law and according to the whim of any one man, and the tyrannies seldom lasted long. Sparta, indeed, never had a tyrant, and she was always ready to increase her power by helping drive out one from any other state.

One of the most famous tyrants was Po-lyc′ra-tes of Samos, who seemed for a long while to be the luckiest man in the world. **Polycrates** He seized the throne in one island after another, and even with **of Samos** the help of Sparta the people could do nothing against him. He built a fleet of one hundred ships, and whenever a galley with a specially rich cargo was heard of, some of these fast-sailing vessels would pursue it and bring back to the tyrant a great load of treasure. Whatever he undertook succeeded, and finally his friend, the king of Egypt, wrote him: "The gods will surely be jealous of your prosperity. Give up, I pray you, whatever you value most highly, that they may not be envious and do you a harm." The thing that Polycrates looked upon as his rarest treasure was a splendid emerald signet ring, and he threw this into the sea. **Story of the** "Surely, the gods will not envy me now," he said to himself **signet ring** regretfully, as he gazed at the place where his ring had disappeared. A few days later, a fisherman brought him a great fish for a present. Behold, when the fish was opened, there lay the emerald ring. When the king of Egypt heard of this, he thought, "The gods refuse his offering. I can no longer be his ally, for certainly some terrible misfortune is about to befall him." The

SIGNET RINGS
(Found in making excavations)

prediction came true, for Polycrates fell into the hands of an enemy, who put him to death by crucifixion.

Another famous tyrant was Di-o-nys'i-us of Syr'a-cuse, who lived more than a century after Polycrates. He was cruel and revengeful, but one pleasant story is told of his rule. A man named Pyth'i-as conspired against him and was sentenced to death. Pythias begged for a few days of freedom, to arrange some business affair. "My friend Da'mon will take my place," he said, "and if I do not return, he will die in my stead." Dionysius scoffed at the idea of such friendship, but he was so curious to see what the result would be that he agreed to the exchange. The time for the execution drew near, but Pythias was not to be seen. At the last moment he appeared, breathless with haste, for some unexpected obstacle had delayed him. The story declares that Dionysius was so moved by this unselfish affection that he pardoned Pythias and begged that he might become a third in their friendship.

The friendship of Damon and Pythias

SUMMARY

Many Greek colonies had been founded.
The oracles were of great value to the colonists.

Poetry and philosophy flourished in the colonies. Lesbos was the home of Alcæus and of Sappho; Samos, of Pythagoras.

The colonizing went on between 750 B. C. and 600 B. C.

Most of the Greek states became oligarchies, then fell into the hands of tyrants. One famous tyrant was Polycrates of Samos. Another, who lived later, was Dionysius of Syracuse.

SUGGESTIONS FOR WRITTEN WORK

A Greek tells why he wishes to become a colonist.

The king of Egypt relates the story of Polycrates.

Dionysius tells about Damon and Pythias.

IX

THE FIRST AND SECOND PERSIAN EXPEDITIONS

In the course of time most of the Greek states overthrew their tyrants. This was fortunate, for in the trouble that was coming **The tyrants** upon them the people of a state needed to stand together, and **overthrown** not to be ruled by some person who cared little for them or the country if only he could keep his position as tyrant.

This trouble was coming from the east. Just across the Ægean Sea was the country of Lydia. Here and in the neighboring territories the Greeks had founded colonies, and as so many of the colonists had come from Athens and other Ionian cities and were, therefore, of Ionian blood, the whole group of settlements became known as I-o'ni-a. These settlements had become prosperous **Ionia** and rich. It was easy to get rich in Lydia. That was the country in which King Mi'das was said to have lived when he received the power to turn into gold whatever he touched, the power which became abhorrent to him when his daughter was turned into a lifeless golden image. People said that the bottom of a river had been changed to gold because the "golden touch" had disappeared when Midas bathed in its waters. However

Crane
KING MIDAS'S DAUGHTER TURNED
INTO GOLD

that may be, the stream certainly did "roll down golden sand." At first the Lydians had not cared especially about their seacoast, and had made no objection to the settlements of the Greeks; but as the time passed they began to realize that a kingdom ought not to be shut away from the sea by people of another nation. "Ionia must at least admit that I am its king," declared the ruler of the Lydians; and he attacked Mi-le'-tus, the largest and richest of the colonial cities. The attack ended peacefully; the city and the kingdom agreed to be good friends.

The next Lydian king was Crœsus. He laid siege to one colony, — but rather gently, so as to do it no real harm, — and soon not only that one but all the Ionian colonies agreed to acknowledge him as their king. Crœsus was the richest ruler in Asia, and he was as generous as he was rich. He admired the Greeks and liked them and was always ready to do them favors. The Spartans once sent to buy gold of him to adorn the statue of a god, and he gave them freely all that they needed. An Athenian had been kind to his envoys, and the grateful king led him into the royal treasure-chamber and told him to take as much gold as he could carry. He was so good to the Del'phi-ans that they made him a citizen of the sacred place. The colonies were not pleased at losing their independence, but they had nothing to fear from so kindly a ruler.

The time soon came, however, when they did have reason to be alarmed. Cy'rus, king of the Persians, had overthrown Me'di-a, the land lying to the eastward of his kingdom, and was ready to attack Lydia. He invited the colonies to join him. Miletus did so, but the others refused. Crœsus was defeated; and then Ionia had to yield. **Ionia yields to Cyrus**

So it was that Greece lost the rich colonies of the Lydian coast; and before many years had passed, the Greeks began to fear for their own homeland. The Persian empire, vast as it was, was not vast enough to satisfy Cyrus's son Cam-by'ses, and when he became ruler he set to work to make it larger. He conquered Phœ-nic'i-a, and then swept along the African coast, conquering Egypt and the Greek colonies lying to the west of it. The next **The conquests of Cambyses**

king, Da-ri'us, was even more ambitious than Cyrus and Cambyses, and as soon as he had quieted some revolts, made a few fine buildings, and laid out some good roads, he, too, set out to enlarge his kingdom. First, he turned to the east, and soon India had become a part of the Persian empire. He had not forgotten the country that lay to

SEAL OF DARIUS
(Representing him in a lion hunt. The inscription is, " I am Darius, the Great King ")

the west, and before long he determined to try his hand in Europe. He had an old grudge against the Scyth'i-ans, who lived in what is now southern Russia, so he started to conquer **Darius** them. He crossed the Bos'pho-rus and marched through **Thrace** and toward the north. He knew the Danube would be in his way, so he had sent his fleet to its mouth with orders to make a bridge of boats across it. Then over the Danube he went in pursuit of the Scythians. He might as well have chased the wind, for they had no towns to be destroyed, and they almost lived on their horses. They had a most exasperating fashion of keeping just in sight of the Persians, but never allowing them to catch up.

SCYTHIAN WAR-
RIOR WITH CLUB

The Scythians were enjoying themselves, but Darius was at his wits' end. Then the provoking Scythians sent him a present, — a mouse, a frog, a bird, and five arrows. "If the Persians are wise," said the envoy, "they can find out the meaning for themselves." "The mouse is of the earth, the frog of the water, the bird of the air, and the arrows signify warfare," mused Darius. "This means that they are about to surrender." But one of his men did not agree. "This is its meaning," he said: "Unless, Persians, ye can turn into birds and fly up into the sky, or become mice and burrow under the ground, or make yourselves frogs and take refuge in the fens, ye will never make escape from this land, but die pierced by our arrows." Darius scorned this interpretation; but one day it came to pass that the Scythians and the Persians were really drawn up in line for battle, when a hare started up, and the Scythians all rushed off in pursuit of the hare. Then said Darius to the inter-

Darius fears the Scyth-ians

SCYTHIAN WARRIOR WITH
SWORD AND SHIELD

preter, "You were right. These Scythians despise us, and we will return to Persia."

They set out on the return, but the Scythians went faster and came first to the bridge of boats. It was guarded by some of the Ionians who had surrendered to Darius. "Break down the bridge," urged the Scythians, "and then you may go home in peace. We will see to it that King Darius never makes war again." The Ionian leaders had been put by Darius in charge of some cities that he had conquered. One of them, Mil-ti'a-des, said, "Let us destroy the bridge, and then Greece will be forever free from the fear of Darius." "No," objected His-ti-æ'us, the ruler of Miletus, "if Darius is slain, we shall no longer be PERSIAN OFFICER in command of his cities." The bridge was not destroyed, and Darius went home in safety. He had not subdued the Scythians, but he had forced many towns in Thrace and Macedonia to submit to him. Indeed, to the north, east, and south of Greece all was in his hands; and to make matters even worse for the little country, the kingdom of Car'-thage, in Africa, was trying to get possession of the island of Sicily.

PERSIAN BODYGUARD

The Greeks of the mother country were alarmed, and the Greeks in Ionia were un- The revolt happy. Still, nothing might have been done of the Ionian if Histiæus, whom Darius insisted upon keep- colonies ing at his court, had not longed to return to Miletus. He said to himself, "If the Ionian colonies would only revolt, perhaps

Darius would send me back to quell them." He contrived to send a message to his son-in-law, saying, "Set a revolt on foot in Ionia." The son-in-law obeyed. Then he crossed the Ægean Sea to learn whether Greece would help on the revolt. Sparta did not care to help Ionian colonies and so strengthen Athens, but Athens could hardly refuse to aid her own colonists. Moreover, she had a little grudge of her own against the Persians because they had received Hippias and done all that they could to make

PERSIAN SOLDIER

Athens and Eubœa aid Ionia

him again tyrant of Athens. The Athenians concluded to send twenty ships. The E-re′tri-ans of Eu-bœ′a, a large island just off the shores of Attica, agreed to help, and so they and the Athenians sailed across the Ægean Sea. The colonists and their allies took Sar′dis, Darius's capital; then so many Persians came to oppose them that they began to be afraid. They hurried on board their ships and went home. They had done enough to make Darius hate them, but not enough to be of much service to the colonists. Swift couriers hastened to Darius. "O king," they cried, "Sardis is taken and burned by the Ionians and the Athenians!" "The Athenians, who are they?" demanded Darius. His counselors told

"Remember the Athenians"

him. He shot an arrow into the air and called, "O Zeus, suffer me to avenge myself on the Athenians!" Then he turned to a slave and gave him this command: "Whenever I seat myself to eat, do you cry aloud thrice, 'O king, remember the Athenians.'"

Darius was not the man to forget his anger, and it was not long before a Persian army was marching through Thrace and a Persian fleet sailing swiftly toward Attica and Eubœa. Mar-do'ni-us, son-in-law of Darius, was in command. The fleet had The first Persian expedition, 492 B. C. to pass a long rocky promontory, at whose end is Mount A'thos with its jagged rocks and precipitous cliffs. When the ships were northeast of this point, a furious storm arose from the northeast and dashed the helpless vessels upon the rocks. So many ships were lost and so many men were drowned that there was nothing for the Persians to do but to turn about and go home.

The first attempt to invade Greece had come to an end, but the slave still cried thrice at every meal, "O king, remember the Athenians!" and Darius soon began to make ready a second time to invade Greece. He did not care to fight just for the sake of fighting, and before making an attack, he sent envoys to the different Grecian states to say, "Darius, the great king, demands that you send him earth and water." All nations knew that to give earth and water was a token of submission. Some of the states yielded, but others, especially Athens and Sparta, were so angry that they forgot to be honorable. The Athenians threw the king's envoys into a chasm where criminals were often flung; the Spartans dropped those who came to them into a deep well and told them to take their fill of earth and water.

Then followed the second Persian expedition. The Persians had no idea of being wrecked on Mount Athos again, and so The second expedition, 490 B. C. they sailed straight across the sea to Eubœa. "Help us!" the Eretrians begged of Attica, and the Athenians sent them troops. They would probably have sent many more had they not learned that the Eretrians were not united. Some were ready to fight to the death; but others only waited for a good chance to betray the city to the Persians, and so win a reward from King Darius. It was not of much use to help such people, and therefore the Athenians went home. The Eretrians fought for a while, then one of them betrayed the city; and now that was in the hands of the Persians.

There would be no trouble in conquering Attica, the Persians thought; so they put chains on their captives, who were to be sold

Persians land at Marathon

as slaves, loaded them into the vessels, and sailed across the straits to Attica. They had on board a man who knew the country well, for it was Hippias himself. "The plain of Mar'a-thon is the best place to land," he had said. "It is wide and level and gives good space to use the cavalry." So on Marathon

PLAIN OF MARATHON
(From a photograph)

the Persians landed. The mountains looked down calmly upon the thousands of soldiers, and Hippias dreamed of being again tyrant of Athens.

But all this while the Athenians were not idle. From each

The allies of the Athenians

one of the tribes that Clisthenes had formed, one thousand men had come, armed and ready for battle. Just beyond the borders of Attica was Pla-tæ'a. Athens had defended Platæa from Thebes, and Platæa was eager to return the favor; therefore through one of the narrow mountain passes there came marching one thousand Platæan soldiers to help their good friends, the Athenians. The Spartans, too, wished to help drive away the Persians; but they believed it unlucky to start for war during the five or six days before the full of the moon; and before the full of the moon had come, the battle of Marathon had been fought.

The most we know of the battle is that the Greeks were drawn up in line in front of the hills; the Persians were between them **The battle of Marathon, 490 B. C.** and the sea; off the shore were the ships and the chains in which the Greeks were to be carried away as slaves if they lost the battle. There were ten times as many Persians as Greeks; but the Greeks were united, and they were fighting for their homes and their freedom. Miltiades, who had urged destroying the Danube bridge, was general. He gave the command. The Greeks rushed forward at full speed and charged the Persian lines. It is no wonder that the invaders stared and for a

PLAN OF BATTLE OF MARATHON

moment almost forgot to fight. "They are madmen," the Persians cried; "see them charge with no bowmen and no cavalry to protect them!" Then the two lines met in deadly combat. The Greeks were strongest in the wings, the Persians at the centre. Near the end of the battle, the Greek wings routed the Persian wings, but the Persian centre broke through the Greek centre. Then the Greek wings faced about and burst upon the Persians, and the Persians ran, across the plain and down the **The Persians retreat** slope of the shore. They splashed through the shallow water and clambered into their vessels as if fiends were after them. They might almost as well have been chased by fiends as by those angry Greeks, who rushed on in mad pursuit through the water and even up to the very gunwales of the Persian ships. "Fire, fire!" they shouted; "bring us fire to burn the galleys!" And before the Persians could get away, the Greeks had captured seven of their vessels

The invaders had gone, but there was not a minute for rest or rejoicing, for the fleet was sailing directly south. "Athens, Athens, they will attack Athens!" was the cry. The weary troops marched straight to Athens and encamped on the banks of the I-lis'sus; and when the Persians found that the city could not be taken by surprise, they turned about and went home.

Then was the time for rejoicing. In one way Marathon was only a little battle; that is, no large numbers of men were engaged in it. In another way it was one of the greatest battles of the world; for if the Greeks had not conquered, the brave, proud, liberty-loving people would have become the slaves of the Persians. Miltiades was the great man of the hour, and the Athenians could not do enough for him. The Spartans had come at a forced

Marathon one of the greatest battles of history

march, hoping to be in time for the battle. Now they could only go to the plain of Marathon, gaze upon the prisoners and the tents full of treasures, and praise the valor of the Athenians. But how should honor be shown to

BATTLE OF MARATHON

After the battle

the valiant warriors who had saved their country? It was the custom of the Greeks to bring home for burial the bodies of those who had fallen in battle, but of the heroes of Marathon they declared, "Let them lie where they fell. Their bodies shall never leave the place of their deeds of valor." So on the plain of Marathon they buried the Greeks who had been slain. They raised over them a mighty mound of earth, and on the mound they planted ten stately marble pillars, whereon was written the name of every Athenian who had fallen in resisting the barbarians. Another great mound was raised in honor of the Platæans. Here, too, pillars were raised, inscribed with the names of the heroes,

GREEK FOOTMAN AT MARATHON

even of the slaves, who had died for the salvation of Greece. Marble columns pass away, they fall and are broken, they are shattered by earthquakes, they are carried to other countries; but a mound of earth remains, and the mounds on the plain of Marathon may be seen to this day. There is, too, another memorial; for in the little villages thereabout the people sometimes waken in the night and fancy that through the stillness they can hear the neighing of horses, the groans of wounded men, and the mighty shouts of victory; and as they stand and peer into the darkness, they imagine that they can see the shadowy forms of the men who fought at Marathon.

SUMMARY

The Asiatic colonies to the east of Greece were called Ionia. They were conquered by the Lydian king, Crœsus, then fell into the hands of Cyrus, king of Persia.

Cambyses, and after him, Darius, wished to enlarge the Persian empire. Darius tried to conquer the Scythians and failed, but made many other conquests in Thrace and Macedonia.

Ionia revolted against Darius, and was aided by the Athenians. Darius sought revenge on the Athenians, but his fleet was wrecked on Mount Athos. So ended the first Persian expedition.

In the second Persian expedition Darius's ships sailed straight to Eubœa, and then aimed at Attica. He was defeated in the battle of Marathon. The heroes of Marathon were honored by mounds of earth and pillars raised on the battlefield.

SUGGESTIONS FOR WRITTEN WORK

An Ionian writes a friend of the conquest by Crœsus.

A Scythian describes the attack of Darius.

Miltiades writes a letter to his wife describing the battle of Marathon.

X

THE GREAT PERSIAN INVASION

WHILE the Athenians were still rejoicing over the victory at Marathon and saying to one another, "At last we are well rid of the Persians," there were some among them who did not feel so sure that their enemies would not come again. The leader of this

**Themis-
tocles**

party was a man named The-mis'to-cles. His father was a Greek, but his mother was a foreigner, and therefore as a boy he was looked down upon by the boys who were of pure Greek blood. He made things somewhat harder for himself because he would not fall into their ways. He thought, for instance, that it was foolish to learn the accomplishments that were taught to them. The story is told that once after some one had given pleasure to a company by his singing, the remark was made rather sneeringly to Themistocles, "We seem to hear no songs from you." "No," he He urges Athens to build ships replied, "I understand nothing of music and song, but I do know how to make a small city into a large one." Themistocles had fought at Marathon, and he believed not only that the Persians would return and with still greater forces, but also that if the Athenians were to defend themselves, they must learn to fight on the water as well as on the land. "Build ships, build ships," he was saying continually.

THEMISTOCLES

The leader of those who were opposed to Themistocles was Ar-is-ti'des, a man so upright that he was often called "the Just." He also had met the Persians at Marathon, and he honestly believed that Themistocles was in the wrong. "It is our victories on land that have made us strong," he said to himself, "and shall we intrust our safety to the perils of the ocean?" He and his party opposed Themistocles so strongly that perhaps not one Aristides opposes Themisto cles new vessel would have been built if war had not broken out between Athens and Æ-gi'na. Ægina was so much better supplied with ships than Athens, and Athens so felt the need of them in this war, that little by little the Athenians began to think that Themistocles might be in the right. At last the opposition between the two parties became so bitter that the matter was brought to the test of ostracism. The story is told that while Aristides stood watching the voters drop their shells and bits of potsherd into the urns, a stranger said to him, "I cannot write. Will you put the name of Aristides on my ostrakon?" "What wrong has he ever done you?" Aristides asked; and the man replied, "None, but I am tired of hearing him called 'the Just.'" Aristides said no more, but quietly wrote his name. The vote was against him, and he went into exile.

Even then the ships were not built at once, for shipbuilding is always expensive, and where the money was to come from was a question. Fortunately, a large sum came into the Athenian treasury just then from some rich silver mines. "Give this money to build a fleet," Themistocles pleaded, and at last the ships were built. Pi-ræ′us, the port of Athens — for the city was four miles from the sea — was fortified, or rather, partially fortified; for before the work was completed the Persians were on their way for a third invasion of Greece.

When the ships of Darius had come home without the plunder and the troops of prisoners that the king had expected, and he learned of the battle of Marathon, he was a very angry sovereign. Twice the Persian forces had crossed into Europe, and twice they had been driven back. They should go again, and he himself would go with them. Those haughty Athenians should learn how kings of Persia treated the insolent tribes that dared oppose them. He began to make ready. He sent to the cities that he had conquered and ordered them to assemble men and horses and ships, and to provide great stores of grain. For three years the preparations went on; then Darius suddenly died.

Xerx′es, son of Darius, became king. He was satisfied with the size of his kingdom, and he would rather have stayed at home. His counselors, however, were of another mind. Mardonius in particular, who had led the first expedition against the Greeks, was eager to show that, even if he had failed once, he was, nevertheless, a skillful general.

Xerxes decided to make the expedition, and he meant that it should succeed. There must be no wrecking of ships on Mount Athos, so he had a canal dug straight across the peninsula. The land forces must cross the Hel'les-pont, and there he had two bridges of boats built. A little later the great king was in a great passion, for a storm had swept away his bridges. He bade his men give the Hellespont three hundred lashes for its insolence in daring to break down his work, and he ordered the heads of the builders to be cut off. Then he did one thing that was decidedly more sensible — he set to work to make stronger bridges. First, boats were anchored side by side until the space between the two shores was filled. Then six enormous cables were stretched from shore to shore, resting on the decks of the vessels. Upon these were laid logs, then planks, and then earth. Everything was firmly fastened; and last of all, a palisade was built on both sides, so high that the horses and cattle could not be frightened by seeing that the water was under them. The second bridge was built in the same fashion.

Xerxes makes a canal and bridges of boats

When the bridges were done, the canal cut, and stores of food deposited in different places along the way that Xerxes intended to take, he marched out from his capital. For a little while he was a badly frightened monarch, for the sun went into eclipse. "What does it mean?" he demanded of his wise men, in terror. "Fear not, O great king," they replied; "the sun gives warning to Greeks, but the moon to Persians. The sun has vanished from the heavens, and so will the cities of the Greeks vanish from the earth." Then the king marched on.

The eclipse of the sun

When the army came to the Hellespont, there stood on the top of a hill a white marble throne which Xerxes had ordered to be made ready for him. He took his seat on the throne. Below him were hundreds of vessels and uncounted thousands of men, the greatest land and sea force that ever came together. Xerxes always enjoyed a spectacle. He gazed and gazed, at the sea, at the shore, and again at the sea; and the thought that was uppermost in the mind of this royal commander was that it was an excellent opportunity for a boat-race! The race was held and greatly delighted the king. He was still more pleased

THE SO-CALLED "THRONE OF XERXES"
(From a photograph)

as he looked again upon his troops. All at once he began to weep. "There came upon me a sudden pity," he said, "when I thought of the shortness of man's life and considered that of all this host, so numerous as it is, not one will be alive when a hundred years are gone by." This was all true, but no efficient commander would have had leisure at such a time for either boat-races or philosophy.

On the following day the invaders were to cross the Hellespont.

Long before light the Persians were burning spices on the bridge of boats and strewing the way with myrtle boughs. They kept close watch of the eastern sky, for the sun was their god, and if it rose clear and bright, they might look for success. When the first rays dazzled their eyes, they rejoiced, and Xerxes poured out an offering of wine from a golden goblet. "O Or'muzd," he cried, "I pray thee that no misfortune may hinder me from

conquest until I have made my way to the uttermost bounda-
ries of Europe." He cast into the Hellespont the golden goblet,
a golden bowl, and a sword; and then the army began
to cross.

This was the most magnificent procession ever seen
in the world. There were the Ten Thousand Immortals,
the special guard of the king, marching steadily and
gravely, with crowns on their heads. One thousand of
them carried spears with golden pomegranates at the
lower end, and nine thousand bore spears tipped with
pomegranates of silver. There were the ten sacred
horses all richly caparisoned. There was the holy
chariot of Ormuzd, the sun-god, drawn by eight milk-
white steeds. So revered was this
chariot that not even the charioteer
was allowed to enter it, but must drive as best
he could walking behind it. After the chariot
of Ormuzd came that of Xerxes, drawn by great
horses. There were Persians and Medes, with
iron coats of mail, bows and arrows, short spears
and daggers, and big wicker shields. There were
As-syr'i-ans with brazen helmets and linen corse-
lets and clubs knotted with iron. There were
Sa'cæ with tall pointed caps; Sa-ran'gi-ans in
garments of the most gorgeous coloring; E-thi-
o'pi-ans of the West, their bodies painted half
red and half white; Ethiopians of the East, who
wore on their heads the scalps of horses, the
ears pricked up and the mane serving as a crest. There were
Col'chi-ans with wooden helmets and little rawhide shields;

FOOTMAN IN XERXES'
ARMY

WARRIOR IN
XERXES' ARMY

Different
countries re-
presented in
Xerxes'
army

Thra'cians with their long cloaks and on their heads the skins of foxes; Cha-lyb'e-ans, whose brazen helmets were made in the shape of an ox's head. There were chariots and horses and camels and servants and long trains of provisions. Everything of metal was burnished and shining; and the Persians, especially, wore so many golden ornaments that their lines fairly glittered.

Over the bridges they went, and for seven long days and nights the people who lived about the Hellespont heard the tramp, tramp of marching feet. Having passed the bridges, the land forces moved on to Do-ris'cus in Thrace, where the ships, too, were to assemble. Here it was that Xerxes numbered his forces. This is the way he did it. Ten thousand men were crowded together in a circle. Then a pen was built just the size of the circle and filled with men. There were enough foot-soldiers to fill it one hundred and seventy times, making 1,700,000. The horsemen were 80,000.

CHARIOT IN XERXES' ARMY

Xerxes drove in his chariot about the plain, from nation to nation. Then he stepped into a galley, and, sitting beneath a golden canopy, he watched the vessels as they passed him in single file. After the first this review must have been rather tiresome, for there were 1207 warships, besides about 3000 smaller vessels and ships of burden.

There seemed to be forces enough to sweep the little country of Greece off the face of the earth. Xerxes sent for a Greek who had been driven by his countrymen from the throne of Sparta, Xerxes' confidence in his army and said, "Dem-a-ra′tus, my opinion is that even if the Greeks were all gathered together, they could not resist my attack but what do you think?" Demaratus asked, "O king, shall I give you a true answer, or do you wish only for a pleasant one?" "Speak the plain truth," bade the king, "and I shall hold you in no less favor." Then Dem-aratus told him that, however it might be with other tribes, the Spartans, at least, would never become his slaves. "If there were only one thousand of them," he

MOUNTED ARCHER IN XERXES' ARMY

declared, "they would not flee, but would come out boldly and meet your whole army in battle." King Xerxes laughed and sent him away with words of kindness.

The army grew larger as it went on, for the tribes that had been conquered by the Persians in the earlier invasions were Feeding the Persian army obliged to furnish soldiers. Long before this, warning had been sent to the towns along the road that they must provide food for the army. They did not dare to refuse, and for many months they had been hard at work making ready. Wheat and barley must be ground, cattle and poultry must be bought and fattened. These were for the army; but the townsfolk knew well that if they would win the favor of Xerxes, they must also prepare an elaborate banquet for him and his friends. On such a banquet one town spent $500,000, and other towns spent nearly as much. The army ate the country bare and actually drank the rivers dry, leaving behind them only little muddy brooks trickling down the empty channels.

Whether to go through the Pass of Tem'pe in Thessaly, or

Xerxes de-
mands sub-
mission of
the Greek
states

another one farther from the shore, was the question. Xerxes went aboard one of his ships and made a short voyage, so that he could see Tempe from the water. He anchored off the Thessa'li-an coast, and stood gazing at the shore. Before him rose mighty cliffs. In the cliffs was a narrow cleft through which a river was flowing into the sea. "Is there no other outlet for the river?" he asked. "None, O king," was the reply, "for Thessaly is girt all about with a circlet of mountains." "They were wise men, then, those Thessalians," said the king, "to submit to me in time. I could easily fill up that gorge and turn the whole country into a lake." Xerxes sailed back to his army; but before going any farther he dispatched heralds to the various states, demanding earth and water. No heralds were sent to either Athens or Sparta, because of the way they had treated those sent previously.

The Greeks had been watching the movements of Xerxes as a

**The Greeks
do not unite**

mouse might watch those of a cat. "He is making vast preparations; he is at Sardis in Lydia; he is at the Hellespont; he has crossed"; such were the reports that came to them. Some states decided at once to yield to the mercy of the Persian king and sent him earth and water. The Athenians knew well that no mercy would be shown them. They knew, too, that there was no hope of success in resisting the Persians if they had to stand alone. Therefore they asked the different states to send envoys to a council to be held at Corinth. Some sent; some did not. The Spartans were looked upon as the best soldiers of Greece, and they would naturally lead the army; but Argos would have nothing to do with any union unless her king could share the command. Thebes would not agree to anything proposed by

Athens. Messengers had also been sent to the larger colonies, asking them to help save the mother country from the barbarians. "If Greece is conquered," they said, "the Persians will then fall upon you. Save yourselves by saving Greece." Ge′lo, tyrant of Syracuse in Sicily, sat listening to the message. He replied, Gelo's attitude "Yes, I will send you two hundred ships of war and twenty-eight thousand men, and I will supply food for the whole army as long as the war lasts; but I, Gelo of Syracuse, must then be leader and commander." "The command belongs to Sparta," declared the messengers. "If you will not follow our lead, send us no troops." "I have forces many times as great as those of Sparta," said Gelo, "but I will yield and be content to command either on sea or on land."

A GREEK COMMANDER

Then the Athenian envoys stood for their own rights. "We are the oldest nation in Greece," they said, "we dwell where we have always dwelt; we have the largest fleet; even at Troy our leader was famous for his skill; and if the Spartans yield the command of the sea to any one, it is ours." Gelo retorted, "You are likely to have more commanders than men. The sooner you return the better."

Athens, Sparta, Platæa, and other states that had agreed to stand together saw that they could hope for no strength but their own. The Athenians sent messengers to Delphi. The oracle was as confusing as the oracles usually were, and the only statement that seemed clear was that the enemy would capture Athens. One line in particular the Athenians discussed over and over. It was, "Safe shall the wooden walls continue for thee and The "wooden walls" thy children." Some recalled the fact that in the early days the Acropolis was fortified by a wooden palisade. "Whatever happens," they said, "we can take refuge on the Acropolis." Themistocles declared that "wooden walls" meant their ships; and finally most of the Athenians came to agree with him.

SUMMARY

Themistocles urged the Athenians to build ships. Aristides was ostracized, and after a time the ships were built.

Darius made ready for a third expedition against Greece. At his death his son Xerxes took his place. He dug a canal across the peninsula of Mount Athos, bridged the Hellespont, and stored food in various places along what was to be his line of march. He halted at the Hellespont, reviewed his fleet, and held a boat-race, then crossed the Hellespont. At Doriscus in Thrace the land and sea forces met. There Xerxes numbered his men. Towns along the way were forced to feed the Persians. Xerxes visited the Pass of Tempe. He demanded earth and water of the Greek states. Some yielded.

The Athenians called a council of states at Corinth. The colonies were also appealed to. Some refused out of jealousy, among them Gelo, tyrant of Syracuse.

The oracle promised safety in the "wooden walls."

SUGGESTIONS FOR WRITTEN WORK

An Athenian tells why he voted against Aristides.
A Persian soldier describes the crossing of the Hellespont.
Two Athenians discuss the meaning of the oracle.

XI

THE GREAT PERSIAN INVASION (*Continued*)

AND now Xerxes was well on his way. The Thracians knew that he would pass through their country first, and they sent messengers to the council at the Isthmus to say, "Men of Greece, we ought not to be left to die in your defense alone and unas- **Where to meet the Persians?** sisted. Send us troops to guard the Pass of Tempe, or we shall make terms with the Persians." An army was sent, but when they learned that there was another pass through which the enemy might enter, they abandoned Tempe and returned to the Isthmus.

The stand against the Persians must be made somewhere, but where was the best place? Of course Xerxes would keep as near the sea as possible. They must, then, find a pass near the coast through which he would be obliged to march, and so narrow that only a few of his men could fight at a time. They decided upon Ther-mop'y-læ because there the mountains jutted out so boldly into the sea that only a narrow roadway

GREEK WARRIORS

was left between them and the water. Here the Greeks took their stand. Le-on'i-das, king of Sparta, was in command. With him were three hundred Spartans whom he had chosen one by one for their courage and patriotism. There were also about **The relative sizes of the two armies** six thousand men from different tribes. This was an absurdly small force to send against the hundreds of thousands of Xerxes; but it was the time of the Olympian games and also of a festival in honor of Apollo. As soon as the festival was over, more men would be sent. No one supposed the struggle at Ther-mopylæ would come so soon; and in any case the state that neglected to honor the gods could expect no good fortune in war.

Xerxes would perhaps have put his men on shipboard and landed them below Thermopylæ; but four hundred of his war-ships had just been wrecked in a storm, and the fleet of the Greeks was guarding the strait at Ar-te-mis'i-um against the others. If he was to enter Greece, he must pass Thermopylæ. This seemed to him a small matter. He had heard that a few men were at the Pass, but he supposed they would soon run away. Indeed, some of them were talking of doing that very thing. "Let us go back to the Isthmus," they urged. "The most we can do is to defend the Peloponnesus." "No," cried Leonidas, "do those of you retreat who wish to retreat; but as for me and my Spartans, we have been sent to guard this Pass, and here we remain."

There was as terrible fighting as the world has ever seen. From morning till night it lasted, and from morning till night of the second day. Then came treachery. A Ma'li-an told Xerxes of a footpath leading over the mountains and around the Pass; and just as it was growing dark this traitor led the Persians out of the camp, across the little river, and up the mountain. The Greek guard at the summit could not see them, as the mountain-side was so thickly covered with oak trees; and they knew no-thing of the coming of the enemy until in the silence of the early morning they heard the tramping of thousands of feet. The little force could only prepare to die; but the enemy rushed by them, eager to surround the Greeks at the Pass.

When Leonidas learned that the path had been discovered, he knew that there was no hope of holding Thermopylæ. "Do you return to the Isthmus if you will," he said to his allies, "but as for me and my Spartans, the laws of our country forbid that we

David

LEONIDAS AT THERMOPYLÆ
(An idealized picture in the Louvre)

should leave the place that we have been sent to guard." The The Thespians also refuse to retreat Thes'pi-ans, too, refused to retreat. The fighting went on, more furiously if possible than before. The Spartans and the Thespians rushed forward into the very midst of the Persian forces. Men were thrust into the sea, were trampled to death by scores and by hundreds. The spears broke, they fought with swords; the swords gave out, they fought with their teeth, with their fists, with stones, with anything that would strike a blow, until they lay dead, buried under heaps of Persian missiles. At this battle, too, the slain were buried where they fell. In memory of the bravery of Leonidas, a marble lion was reared at the entrance of the Pass. Pillars were set up in honor of the soldiers. Upon one was written, —

> "Here did four thousand men from Pe'lops's land
> Against three hundred myriads bravely stand."

Another was in honor of the Spartans alone. Its inscription was, —

> "Go, stranger, and to Lac-e-dæ'mon tell
> That here, obeying her behests, we fell."

Simonides, sixth and fifth centuries B. C.

This was written by Si-mon'i-des, a poet of Ce'os, one of the Cyc'la-des. He could write such strong lines as these, in which every word counts, and he could also write so gracefully and tenderly that his friends used to call him *the sweet poet*. One of his sayings seemed to people so true that it has been famous through all the centuries since he died. It is: "Poetry is vocal painting, as painting is silent poetry."

While the famous little band of Greeks were doing their best to hold back the Persian forces at Thermopylæ, the Greek ships were also at work. They were keeping the Persian fleet from entering the Eu-ri'pus, the strait that lies between Eubœa and the mainland. The Persians thought it would be a good move to send two hundred of their ships around Eubœa and up the Euripus from the south. "Then we shall have the Greek ships shut into the strait," they said, "and with our great fleet it will be easy to destroy them all." They sent the two hundred ships,

The naval battle at Artemisium, 480 B. C.

but soon a storm wrecked every one of them. For one day, two days, three days, the naval battle went on, the Persians trying to press through the strait at Artemisium, and the Greeks holding them back. Just at evening of the third day there came a swiftly sailing vessel that had been watching affairs at Thermopylæ; and now the men on board the Greek ships learned that the Pass was lost, and that the Persians were marching on toward Athens. There was no reason then for guarding the strait; it was far better to sail through the Euripus toward the south. The Greek admiral was a Spartan, but Themistocles commanded the ships of Athens. The winds had fought for the Greeks, and now he meant to make the earth speak for them. Wherever there was a good chance, he sent men to cut on the rocks inscriptions which would be read by the Ionians in Xerxes' army. "Men of Ionia," they said, "come over to our side if possible; if you cannot do this, we pray you stand aloof from the contest, or at least fight backwardly." Themistocles thought that, even if the Ionians did not see these inscriptions, they would surely be read by some of the Persians, and that Xerxes would not venture to use the Ionian aid in the sea-fights. The Greek fleet then sailed around Su'ni-um, the southern point of Attica, and anchored between Athens and the island of Salamis.

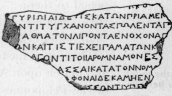

GREEK WRITING ON STONE

The Persians were aiming at Athens, but a little west of their line of march lay Delphi, and there was the temple of Apollo, fairly crowded with treasures. They could not pass that by; so part of the army left the coast and turned to the westward. The Delphians were in despair. "O Apollo," they prayed, "tell us, we beseech thee, what shall we do with thy holy treasures! Shall we bury them in the ground, or carry them away to some other country?" "Fear not," was the reply, "Apollo needs no help to protect his own." Then most of the Delphians departed from the city with the women and children. It was reported by those who remained that the sacred armor of Apollo was moved, but by no man's hands, from the inner shrine and laid in front of the temple. However that may be, there was certainly a terrific thunderstorm. From Mount Parnassus two immense crags split

Strategy of Themistocles

The defense of Delphi

off and rolled down upon the Persian hosts, and by their weight many were crushed. It is no wonder that the barbarians fled in terror from this and the resistance of even the few Delphians, or that in their alarm they told marvelous tales of what had happened to them. "They with whom we fought were not mortal," they declared; "they were armed warriors with stature more than human, who burst upon us and slew some of us."

Athens left to her fate

These men hastened into Bœotia to join the rest of the army and march upon Athens; and Athens was helpless, for the Greeks of the Peloponnesus had quietly abandoned her to her fate and were working night and day to build a high wall across the Isthmus to keep the Persians from attacking their own cities.

Athens had done all that she could to unite the Grecian states. She had planned the council at the Isthmus; she had not asked for control of the army; and although she had many more ships than all the other states, she had allowed the command of the fleet to go into the hands of the Spartans. Now she was abandoned by the rest of Greece. Her only encouragement lay in that one line of the oracle, "Safe shall the wooden walls continue for thee and thy children"; and the citizens could not agree upon

SALAMIS FROM ACROSS THE BAY
(From a photograph)

Advice of the oracle

the meaning of that. Another line that puzzled them greatly was this: "Holy Salamis, thou shalt destroy the offspring of women." Themistocles insisted that the "offspring of women" meant the

Persians. "If it had meant the Greeks," he urged, "the oracle would not have called Salamis 'holy,' but rather 'luckless'; and surely it must mean that at Salamis the Persians will meet some terrible disaster." Whatever the oracle might mean, it was plain that the city could not be saved. Then began a rushing to and fro, a crowding of the women and children into the boats, and a hurrying over the water to safer places. They were hardly out of sight of Athens before the Persians swept down upon it. They overthrew and plundered and burned, till little remained but piles of smoking ruins.

The only hope of the Greeks lay in Salamis and in Themistocles. "We will fight the enemy at the Isthmus," declared the men of the Peloponnesus, "and then if we are defeated, we can retreat to our homes." Themistocles pleaded with them to alter their decision. "We can meet the Persians in the narrow strait at Salamis," he said, "and then it will not matter how many ships they have, for there will be room for them to use only a few. A victory here will defend the Peloponnesus as much as one at the Isthmus; and it is at Salamis that the god has promised us a victory." Here a Corinthian broke in upon him exclaiming, "You are only a man without a city! Show us of what state you are an envoy." Themistocles had kept his temper through other provoking speeches, but now he burst out against his opponents. "No country!" he exclaimed. "I have two hundred ships at my command all ready for battle. What state of Greece can resist me if I choose to make a descent upon it? Be persuaded by my words. If not, we will take our families and make homes for ourselves in Italy. When you have lost us as allies, you will remember what I have said."

The states were beginning to recognize the strength of the

Shall the Persians be met at Salamis?

Threat of Themistocles

Athenians, and had no wish to lose them. They finally voted to meet the Persians at Salamis; but the men of the Peloponnesus still objected. "That is good for the Athenians," they grumbled, "but no gain to us." They succeeded in having another council called, and Themistocles saw that the vote would be changed.

He uses a trick

He made up his mind to use a trick. He sent to the Persians a faithful slave, who was to say, "An Athenian commander who wishes you well sends you this message: 'The Greeks are divided. Some will oppose you and some will join your side. Now is your chance to win a glorious victory.'" Then he slipped back into the council room. The discussion went on till long after midnight.

The message of Aristides

In the midst of it a message was brought to Themistocles: "There is one without who would speak to you." It was Aristides, returned from banishment, for all those who were banished had been recalled lest they should join the Persians. He was eager to help his rival win glory and honor if only Greece might be saved. "The Persian ships are at the entrance of the strait," he whispered. Themistocles saw that the enemy had fallen into his trap and that now the Greeks would be forced to fight, whether they wished it or not.

In the morning the battle of Salamis began. The line of Greek ships stretched across from Salamis to Attica. Farther south, at the entrance of the strait, lay the Persian vessels.

The battle of Salamis, 480 B. C.

Over on the Attic shore, high up on a hill that overlooked the strait, sat Xerxes on his throne, ready to watch every movement. All day long the battle raged. The Persians had so many ships that they got into one another's way. They drifted helplessly about with broken oars and rudders gone. The Greeks sank one after another; they chased the enemy out of the strait; they even sailed around the Persian ships and attacked them from the other side. When

BATTLE OF SALAMIS

Kaulbach

night came, the Greeks had won the victory. They had won more than a single naval battle, for Xerxes had already started for home, sailing as fast as a ship could carry him, for fear the Greeks should break down the bridges over the Hellespont before his troops could march across it. He was disappointed and tired of the whole undertaking and was quite ready to listen to his general Mardonius. "You have done what you wished," Mardonius declared, "you have punished Athens, and may well return to Persia. Leave me with three hundred thousand men, and I can soon conquer the rest of Greece."

The way that Mardonius set about this conquest was by trying to bribe Athens to join with him. "Xerxes will forgive what is past," he said. "He will build you temples, help you to win land,

Xerxes returns to Persia

Mardonius
plans to con-
quer Greece and leave you free, if you will become our allies." And the Athenians replied, "So long as the sun holds on his way in the heavens,
the Athenians will never come to terms with Xerxes." Then
Mardonius marched straight to Athens. The land was there and

THE VICTORS OF SALAMIS

Gormon

the partially rebuilt houses; but a second time the Athenians had
fled from the city; they were all at Salamis.

For some time the states of the Peloponnesus seemed to care
for nothing but their own safety; but at last they saw that even
to save themselves they must help to oppose Mardonius. They
The battle of
Platæa, 479
B. C. pursued him into Bœotia. Then came a furious battle at Platæa,
and Mardonius was slain. What were left of the Persian ships
had gone to Samos and were keeping close watch of the Ionian
colonies, for it was plain that they meant to free themselves as
soon as they were able. The Greek ships were at De'los. To them

three men came secretly from Samos. "Come and help the Ionians to become free," they pleaded. "You can easily drive back the barbarians, for their ships are no match for yours. The moment you are in sight, the Ionians will revolt." The Greeks decided to sail for Ionia. They expected a naval battle, but they found it would have to be fought on dry land, for the Persians had drawn their ships up on the beach near Myc'a-le in Ionia and built around them a wall of logs and stones. When the Greeks saw this, they went ashore. The barbarians were soon routed, and the Ionian colonies joined the league of Grecian states. This was the battle of Mycale, and it was fought on the same day as the battle of Platæa. So it was that Greece was freed from the fear of the Persians; for never again did a Persian army set foot on Grecian soil.

The battle of Mycale, 479 B. C.

SUMMARY

Thermopylæ was chosen as the place to oppose the Persians, and there a terrible battle took place. The dead were buried where they fell. Simonides wrote the inscription on the pillar raised in honor of the Spartans.

The Greek ships defended the Euripus till Thermopylæ was lost. Themistocles left messages on the rocks to the Ionians.

The Persians marched to Delphi, but were driven away by a thunderstorm.

Athens was abandoned by the other Greeks to her fate. The Athenians had to flee from their city, which was burned by the Persians.

After much discussion the Greeks agreed to meet the Persians at Salamis. Themistocles tricked the Persians into making an attack. The Greeks were victorious, and Xerxes started for home.

Mardonius failed to win the Athenians by bribes, and again they were driven from their city.

A fierce battle was fought at Platæa, and Mardonius was slain. The Persian ships retreated to Samos. At the request of the Samians the Greek ships sailed to Ionia and routed the Persians at Mycale.

SUGGESTIONS FOR WRITTEN WORK

Xerxes tells what he expects to do at Thermopylæ.

One of Themistocles's men tells about cutting the inscriptions on the rocks.

A Persian soldier describes what happened at Delphi.

XII

AFTER THE PERSIAN WAR

The honors and treasure of Salamis

AFTER the Greeks had won a battle it was their custom to give prizes to the state and to the commander that had done most to bring about the victory. It seems plain enough that the honors of

VICTORS RETURNING FROM WAR   *Flaxman*

Salamis should have been given to Attica and to Themistocles; but the Peloponnesus was jealous of Attica, and therefore the first state prize was given to Ægina. The attempt to choose the most valiant leader was rather amusing, for each commander gave Themistocles the second place, but wrote his own name for the first. In dividing the treasure the gods were not forgotten. Three ships of war were dedicated to them. One tenth of the spoils went to Delphi, and The gods remembered of this was made a statue of Apollo three times as tall as a man, and holding in one hand the prow of a vessel. After Platæa the tents abandoned by the Persians were found to be fairly ablaze with treasures. There were bowls and goblets, and even kettles, of solid gold; there were couches covered with plates of gold; there were golden bracelets and chains; and there were swords and scimitars with golden handles. As for gorgeously embroidered cloaks and curtains and carpets, they were so common that no one made any account of them. Of this, too, the gods had their full share. Of the part that went to Delphi a golden tripod was made, standing upon a closely coiled three-headed serpent of bronze. For many years after the battle, the Platæans who roamed over the field used to find treasures of gold and silver that had not been noticed at first. Which state should have the prize for valor at Platæa was a hard question, for both Athens and Sparta demanded it. To settle the dispute it was decided to give it to Platæa. Here temples were built to Athene and to Zeus. An oracle declared that the sacred fires of Platæa were no longer holy, because they had been polluted by the barbarians. They were all put out, and a swift runner brought coals from Delphi, by which they were kindled afresh. The Greeks agreed that the Platæan Platæa is consecrated to the gods land should ever afterward be looked upon as sacred ground, and that it should be the duty of the Platæans to offer once a year a sacrifice in memory of the soldiers who had died on their soil. This was kept up for at least three centuries. When the day had come, the trumpets sounded the battle-call early in

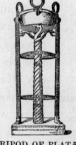

TRIPOD OF PLATÆA, RESTORED

(Made of the gold found on the battlefield of Platæa)

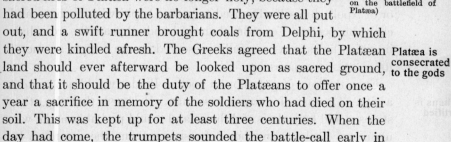

The Platæan
memorial to
the dead sol-
diers
the morning. Then the procession set out. This was formed of
freeborn young men bearing oils and perfumes and milk and
honey. With them went a black bull, and also chariots filled
with myrtle wreaths and branches. Last of all walked the
archon, with flowing purple robe, sword, and watering-pot. On
the monuments of the heroes were little pillars on which their
friends used to place flowers. These the archon washed with his
own hands and rubbed with perfume. He sacrificed the bull,
and distributed the myrtle. Then he filled a bowl with wine and
poured out an offering, saying, "I present this bowl to the men
who died for the liberties of Greece."

At the beginning of the war, when the Spartans claimed the
command of the navy, Themistocles said to the Athenians,
"Behave like men during the war, and when it is over, the
Greeks will yield you the superiority." The war was now over,
and his words had come true; for whatever the other states might
say, they knew well that the Athenians were the leading people
Pindar, sixth
and fifth
centuries
B. C.
of Greece. The poets had always loved Athens. Pin'dar, Theban
as he was, could hardly mention the name of the city without
calling her "glorious," or "beloved," or "renowned." In one
way Pindar belonged not only to Thebes but to all Greece, for
much of his composition was in honor of the victors at the games
or of Apollo himself. He used to go to Delphi with his harp and
chant his poetry. For more than six hundred years the iron chair
in which he sat was carefully preserved in the temple as one of
its greatest treasures.

Even the love of so famous a poet as Pindar would not protect
Athens is
fortified
a city. Themistocles was a wise man. He knew that the other
states would be jealous of Athens, and would probably make war
upon her. To have any hope of resisting them, the city must be

the strongest in the land. It was now in ruins. Much of the wall had been torn down, and the Athenians were scattered about in different places, wherever they had found a refuge. They were glad to return, even to the heaps of ashes and stones that alone remained of their homes; and they set about rebuilding their houses bravely and cheerfully. There was other work, however, that needed to be done even before house-building. In that warm climate it was no great hardship to live out of doors for a while, and Themistocles told them that the wall ought to be built first. They agreed to do this and to follow his plan of making it seven miles long, inclosing the Acropolis and enough land to take in all the country folk if any attack was made upon Attica.

The Spartans were not pleased. They sent envoys to the Athenians to remind them that Sparta had no walls. " It is not well for any Greek city to wall itself in," they protested; "for if invaders should come, they would perhaps get possession of it and be so well protected by the walls that they could sally forth and overcome one state after another at their leisure." Themistocles replied thoughtfully, "There is certainly much reason in what you say, and we will send envoys to Sparta to discuss this matter with you more fully." The Spartans had always liked Themistocles, and now they went home content.

Sparta objects to the Athenian wall

Then the wily leader told the Athenians his plan. The wall must be built without an instant's delay. They set to work, using not only blocks of stone from the ruined houses and temples, but even tombstones. The women worked like men, and even the help of a child who could bring a handful of earth or pass a tool to a workman was welcome. The labor went on, night and day. Themistocles and two others had been appointed envoys to the Spartans, and after waiting as long as he dared, Themisto-

The craft of Themistocles

cles went to Sparta. He told the people that the other two had
been detained, but would soon appear, and then the whole
matter could easily be arranged. While they were waiting, the
Spartans began to hear rumors that the Athenian walls were
rising rapidly. "What does this mean?" they demanded of

TOMBSTONE FOUND IN THE
RUINS OF WALL BUILT BY
THEMISTOCLES

Themistocles. "Do not put faith in
idle rumors," he replied. "Send envoys to Athens, and then you can
learn the truth for yourselves."

Meanwhile the other two envoys
from Athens had come to Sparta, and
had told Themistocles that the walls
were already high enough to serve as
a defense. He had made sure of a
safe return by sending word to the
Athenians: "Keep the Spartans as
hostages until I and the other envoys are safe at home." So he told
the Spartans that Athens must do

what she thought best for her own interest. "If you and your
allies think no Greek city should have walls, let them begin by
tearing down their own." The Spartans were angry, but they
were helpless, and the Athenians completed their wall.

The events of the war had made it clear that Athens ought
to be strong, not only on land but also on the water. She must
have a large fleet and she must also have a safe harbor that
would protect her ships from storm or the attack of an enemy.
Pha-le'rum was the old harbor, but even before the war Themis-

tocles had fixed his eyes upon the harbor of Piræus, four or five
miles from Athens, and had begun to fortify it. This harbor was

a basin large enough to hold three hundred ships. Around it curved a peninsula ending in a mass of rock, so that only a narrow entrance was left. Along this peninsula the Athenians built seven miles of wall. And what a wall it was! Thirty feet high, wide enough for two chariots to drive abreast, and all made of solid stone clamped together with iron.

All this was done between 479 and 477 B. C. Other work was also going on during that time, for in one way the Persian war **The Greeks** had not yet come to an end. The Ionian colonies had been freed **capture** at the time of the battle of Mycale, but the Persians held many **Byzantium** other places along the coast of Asia Minor and Thrace. The most important was By-zan'ti-um, now Con-stan-ti-no'ple. There could be no safety so long as the Persians had strongholds near

Greece, where they could assemble troops and ships, and from which they could sally forth to attack the Greeks. Moreover, Greece needed more grain than she could raise. It had been brought to her

MODERN VIEW OF THE PIRÆUS
(From a photograph)

through the Pro-pon'tis, which is now the Sea of Mar'mo-ra; but while the Persians held Byzantium, no grain could find its way to Greece from that direction. A fleet was now sent out which besieged and captured Byzantium.

Aristides commanded the Athenian vessels; but the Spartan Pau-sa'ni-as, who had led the troops at Platæa, was admiral of **Pausanias** the fleet. If Pausanias had been killed at Platæa, he would have

His downfall been remembered as a brave and patriotic general; now he is remembered as a traitor. After the victory at Platæa, he behaved as if no one but himself had struck a blow; and after the capture of Byzantium, he seemed to think himself the greatest man in the world. Greece was a small country for so mighty a general, he thought; his glory would be much better appreciated in the vast realm of Persia. He set to work to win the regard of Xerxes by sending back to him the men of highest rank who had been captured at Byzantium. Worse than that, he sent with them a letter to Xerxes saying in effect, "If you will give me your daughter in marriage, I will conquer Greece for you." Xerxes did not promise to give his daughter, but he agreed to provide whatever men and money might be needed for the conquest. Then Pausanias lost his senses completely. He began to act as if he were a high official of Persia. There was no more Spartan simplicity for him; he wore the richest of Persian dress and lived as luxuriously as possible. When Aristides objected, he turned away, saying that he had no time to listen to him.

When the Spartans heard of Pausanias's behavior, they ordered him to come home. They could not prove that he was plotting treason, but after a while it was shown that he was arousing the Helots to rise against their masters. He fled to a room adjoining the temple of Athene, and there was shut in by the Spartans, to starve. To win Athene's forgiveness for the pollution of her temple, they presented her with two bronze statues.

Themistocles flees to Persia The last years of Themistocles's life were hardly more honorable than those of Pausanias. After his trickery in connection with the walls of Athens, the Spartans hated him; and it is possible that they had something to do with his ostracism, which occurred about a year before the death of Pausanias. There was reason to believe that he had joined in Pausanias's plot to conquer Greece for the Persians. It was well known that he had taken bribes; and people began to talk about his advice at the close of the war, not to pursue Xerxes or destroy the Hellespont bridge. "It is true **He appeals** that he said it would be better to get the Persians out of Europe **to Xerxes** and then attack them in Asia," they reasoned; "but it would be easy for him to persuade Xerxes that this plan was urged as a favor to him." This was exactly what Themistocles was doing.

He had fled from one place to another, and finally to the court of Xerxes. He reminded the king of this former favor, and ended his appeal with, "If you destroy me, you destroy the enemy of Greece." The king had not thought of destroying him. He was delighted to have so brilliant a man at his court, and he exclaimed, "May the spirit of evil ever put it into the hearts of my enemies to banish their greatest men!" Three times that night he started up in his sleep, crying, "I have Themistocles the Athenian."

Themistocles became a great favorite of the king, and learned Persian, that they might talk together without an interpreter. Three cities were put into

GREEK SOLDIER

his hands to provide him with "bread, wine, and meat" — which seems to have meant that he was free to get as much from them as possible. He spent his last years in luxury and idleness. Finally the king asked him to lead an expedition against the fleet of the Greeks. He could not make up his mind to do this; yet he could not refuse the king. He decided that the only way of **His unhappy** escape was to take his own life. So died the man whom the **end** Greeks had so greatly admired that, when he appeared at the Olympian games, the whole vast assembly forgot the contests

and turned to gaze upon him and point him out to those who did
not recognize him.

Themistocles was a most able man and he did much for Athens
and for all Greece; but even in the days of his greatest glory
the Greeks never trusted him as they did Aristides. He once told
the Athenians that he had a plan for making their city the most
powerful in Greece, but that he could not tell it to so large an assembly. "Tell it to Aristides," the people bade. "If he approves,
it shall be carried out." Aristides reported that the plan would
indeed give Athens the first place among the Greeks, but that
it was grossly treacherous; and the matter was dropped at once.

**Aristides
was trusted
to the last**

When Pausanias was recalled, the command of the fleet fell
into the hands of Aristides. He founded the famous De'li-an

BRONZE COINS BEARING FIGURE OF
THEMISTOCLES
(Made in his honor after the battle of Salamis)

League, so called because the meetings
were held at Delos, and there the
money of the League was kept. The
object of this association was to free
the Greek cities that were still in the
power of the Persians, and to keep
the Ægean Sea free from pirates.
Nearly all the cities on the islands and on the northern and
eastern shores of the Ægean Sea joined the League. Athens was
to be the leader in the association, but was to have no more power
than the other members. How much each state was to contribute
was left to Aristides to decide. Another thing that Aristides did
for Athens was to increase the power of the fourth class of citizens. By his influence a law was passed allowing members of this
class to be chosen as magistrates. A few years after founding the
Delian League Aristides died. He had had every opportunity to
become rich by taking bribes, yet he died a poor man. The state

**He founded
the Delian
League**

built his tomb and cared for his children and grandchildren. He was a wise statesman and a skillful general, but greater than these titles is that by which he will always be remembered, "the Just."

When Aristides gave up the command of the fleet, it passed into the hands of a man after his own heart, Ci'mon, the son of **Cimon** Miltiades. It was rumored in Greece that the Persians were bringing their ships and men together in large numbers at the mouth of the Eu-rym'e-don in Pam-phyl'i-a. That looked as if they were planning another invasion of Greece. Cimon sailed straight to Pamphylia and found the Persian fleet hovering about the mouth of the river. They expected eighty more vessels,

ATHENIAN BALLOTS
(They were of bronze, and bore the inscription, "Ballot of the public vote")

and did not care to fight till these ships had come. Unfortunately **The battle of** for them, Cimon did not ask what they preferred, but attacked them **the Euryme** **don, 466 B.C** on the instant. The men fled from the ships and made for the shore. There lay the camp of the Persian army; but Cimon and his men burst upon it like a whirlwind. After some hard fighting the Greeks won the day. They had captured two hundred ships and were victors on both sea and land. Most men would have been satisfied with two victories in one day, but Cimon did not propose to go home until he had met those other eighty vessels. He set out on a ship hunt, found them, fought with them, and soon he had won his third victory. The Persians in their flight had left an immense amount of treasure behind them. The

Greeks packed this into their vessels and started for home. "I love to enrich my country at the expense of its enemies," Cimon once said; and Athens was indeed enriched with these loads of treasure.

All this while Athens was becoming stronger, partly because **Athens becomes tyrant of the League** of the Delian League. This was constantly growing, for as soon as a city was freed, it became a member of the association. When the League was founded, it was agreed that the smaller states should pay their share of the expenses in money and the larger ones in ships. Gradually, even many of the larger ones found it less trouble to pay in money. Athens had not the least objection. She took the money, built the ships, and added them to her navy. At length the treasury was removed from Delos to Athens, on the ground that it was not safe from the barbarians at Delos. It was some time before the other members realized that, although Athens was protecting them, they were growing poorer and weaker while she was growing richer and stronger. One after another attempted to leave the League, but Athens would not permit this, and obliged them to pay a greater tribute. So it was that the League, which had been at first an association of states, became an empire with Athens as its tyrant-ruler.

Of course this did not please Sparta, and she would gladly have sent an army against her Attic neighbor. Instead of that, she had to send envoys and beg meekly, "O Athens, will you not come and help us?" Sparta was indeed in trouble. First, she was so shaken by earthquakes that only five houses in the **The third Messenian War, 464-- 456 B.C.** city were left standing and thousands of people were killed. This was a good time for the Helots to rebel, and they attacked Sparta. They were repulsed, but the Messenians now revolted, and they were not so easily suppressed. They shut themselves up in Ithome in Messenia, in which their ancestors had once stood against their Spartan masters. The Spartans were not wise in carrying on sieges, neither were the other Peloponnesian cities, but Athens had had much experience in that line; therefore Sparta con- Sparta appeals to Athens cluded to appeal to Athens. The Athenians had not forgotten the time when they had asked Sparta for help and she had shown

so little sympathy for them in their trouble. "Let us refuse," urged one party in Athens. The other party argued, "No, let not Greece be lamed and Athens deprived of her yoke-fellow." Cimon was the leader of this second party. It seemed to him far more reasonable for the Greek states to fight Persia than to quarrel with one another. The Athenians were proud of Cimon, and he had no great difficulty in persuading them to allow him to go to Messenia, to help the Spartans. But when the Spartans saw the force of four thousand men, with the greatest

THE "TORTOISE"
(A means of scaling a wall)

Athenian commander at their head, they began to suspect some trick. Ithome did not fall at once, as they had expected, and then they felt sure that Cimon had plotted with the Messenians to overthrow their state. They told him abruptly that they The Athenians insulted had no need of him and his forces and he might go home, although they asked the troops from the other cities to stay and help them. The Athenians were indignant at such an in-

Cimon blamed

sult. They wanted to blame some one, and their wrath fell upon the popular commander. "He always admired the Spartans," said one. "He named one of his children Lac-e-dæ-mo'ni-us," said another. "And when any of the allies did not please him, he was always saying that the Spartans would not have done so," another added. At length Cimon was ostracized, as Aristides and Themistocles had been. Sparta finally subdued the Messenians and drove them from the Peloponnesus, but Athens arranged for them to live at Nau-pac'tus. It was convenient for her to have an allied settlement on the northern side of the Gulf of Corinth; but this act did not make Sparta feel any more friendly.

The power of Athens increases

PERICLES
(In the British Museum, London)

Many of the Athenians had come to the conclusion before this that there was no use in trying to keep on good terms with Sparta, that war between the two states must come some day, and that the best course for Athens was to make herself as strong as possible. The leader of this party was named Per'i-cles. He now became the most popular man in Athens, and the Athenians were ready to

Pericles

do whatever he advised. They made an alliance with Argos, then with Megara. This was coming to the very gates of the Spartans. The people of the Peloponnesus were not pleased, but the Athenians cared little whether they were pleased or not. They kept on making alliances and winning battles whenever matters came to **Athens be-comes a mighty city** battle, until the influence of Athens extended from Thermopylæ to the Isthmus, and as the head of the Delian League, or rather the Delian empire, she controlled also the cities and islands of the Ægean Sea.

Athens was mighty on the land and mighty on the sea. She had a strongly walled city, and she had a perfectly protected

ATHENS, RESTORED

(In the distance may be seen the Acropolis, and beyond it mountains in Argolis. In the foreground are the city walls and a bridge over the Ilyssus)

harbor. Only one thing was needed, and that was a way of going from the city to the harbor in safety. To bring this about, two **The building of the Long Walls** monstrous walls were built between the city and the sea, taking in not only the port of Piræus but also the old harbor of Phale-rum. After a while a third wall was built, running between Athens and Piræus. These were not common walls, for they were sixty feet in height, and wide enough for two chariots to drive abreast. So long as Athens held the walls, she could not be shut from the sea. Her ships could supply her with food, and it seemed as if at last a city had been made so strong that it could not be conquered.

The power of Athens was at its height, but trouble soon came to her. At almost the same time several of the states subject to her revolted, and a Spartan army ventured into Attica, and began to kill, burn, and destroy. It was fortunate for Athens that she had so wise a leader as Pericles. He saw that, powerful as Athens was, she could not suppress these revolts and fight Sparta **The Peace of** at the same time. He made a peace with Sparta, which was to **Pericles** last thirty years, called the Peace of Pericles; but in order to induce the Spartans to agree to it, Athens had to agree to give up all that she had gained in the Peloponnesus. This ended the possibility that Athens might some day control all Greece. She might have as strong a navy as she chose, but it was plain that she would never be permitted to rule the Greeks of the motherland as she ruled those of the Ægean.

SUMMARY

The treasures of Salamis were shared between the victors and the gods.

Platæa was set apart as sacred ground.

The Athenians became the leaders of Greece. Even the Theban Pindar loved Athens. She was now surrounded by a wall and Piræus was fortified.

The Greeks captured Byzantium.

The attempts of Pausanias to win favor with Xerxes resulted in his downfall.

Themistocles ended his life at the Persian court.

Aristides founded the Delian League to free Greek cities from Persia. He will always be remembered as " the Just."

The command of the fleet fell into the hands of Cimon. He overcame the Persian fleet at the mouth of the Eurymedon, and also the Persian camp, then won a victory over some Persian ships.

Athens was growing stronger, partly because of the Delian League. Sparta was not pleased, but a revolt of the Messenians forced her to ask Athens for aid. The Spartans insulted the Athenian troops. The Athenians foolishly blamed Cimon, and he was ostracized. By invitation of Athens, the Messenians made their home at Naupactus.

Pericles became the chief man at Athens.

Walls were built from Athens to Piræus.

Several states revolted against Athens.

The Peace of Pericles was made, but Athens had to give up what she had gained in the Peloponnesus.

SUGGESTIONS FOR WRITTEN WORK

An account of the division of the spoils of the battle of Salamis.

One of the Spartans tells how Themistocles deceived them about the Athenian walls.

Aristides tells a friend about his plan for forming the Delian League.

XIII

THE AGE OF PERICLES

The reforms of Pericles PERICLES still hoped that the time would come when Greece would be ruled by Athens, although he believed that Sparta's jealousy would some day lead to war. Meanwhile there would be peace between the two states for some years, and he set to work to make his city both beautiful and powerful. The gov-

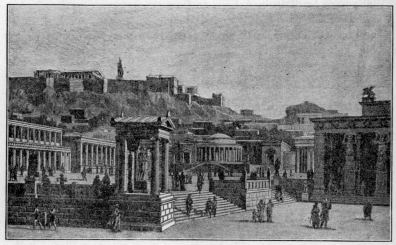

Bühlmann

MARKET-PLACE OF ATHENS, RESTORED
(The Acropolis rises to the left, in the background)

The poorest man eligible to office ernment had come more and more into the hands of the people, until now there was no office to which the poorest man might not be elected. In order that such a man might be able to leave his work to serve the state, Pericles brought it about that those who held the various offices should be paid, and also those who served in the army or navy, or as jurymen. There were several thousand of these jurymen, and all but the gravest offenses were judged

Officials and soldiers paid

BUILDING A TEMPLE

Schinckel

by them. Sometimes hundreds of jurors sat on a single case. So it came about that for one service or another many thousand Athenians were receiving money from the state. The general assembly agreed to all these changes. They could not help seeing that Pericles was working, not for his own glory, but for that of his city; and he was so reasonable and could state his reasons so clearly, that the people fell in with whatever he proposed. He had more power than any king ever possessed; but this was not because the people were afraid of him, but because he was so skillful in war, so wise in peace, and, above all, so thoroughly unselfish. Of course he had enemies, but the greater part of the Athenians looked upon him as the ideal Greek.

The great power of Pericles

Pericles was not only a good soldier and statesman, but he was a lover of what was beautiful. All the Greeks, indeed, loved beauty; they loved it as people love fresh air and sunshine. To have ugly things around them made them uncomfortable; they felt stifled and gloomy. Long before this they had had beautiful buildings and statues, for there had been great artists in Greece for many years; but Pericles planned to cover the Acropolis with a group of temples that should be the masterpieces of Grecian architecture. The noblest of them all was the Par'the-non, a magnificent structure of the purest white marble, sacred to Athene. It had marble columns around it, for the Greeks could not im-

The Parthe-non

PARTHENON, RESTORED

The three styles of columns

agine a great temple without columns. There were three kinds to choose from. First, there was the Co-rin'thi-an, which looks as if the top of the column were surrounded with a cluster of marble leaves most exquisitely carved; and, indeed, it is said that this style really was suggested to the artist by some one's dropping a basket into a cluster of acanthus leaves. The second was the Ionic, whose top, or capital, is carved into two coils, a little like snail-shells. And, third, there was the Dor'ic, which has a plain, solid capital. The Doric always looks simple and strong; and this was what Pericles chose for the Parthenon. Within the building

was a statue of Athene, thirty-nine feet high. This was made
of ivory, the drapery was of gold, and the pupils of the eyes

were probably made
of jewels. In one hand
was a statue of Vic-
tory, and in the other
a spear and a shield.
Beside Athene coiled
a serpent, represent-
ing Wisdom. Within
the row of columns
was a frieze, or band
of sculpture, running
around the building.
This showed the fa-
mous procession that

SECTION OF THE PARTHENON FRIEZE
(In the centre are the gods Poseidon and Apollo, and the Goddess Demeter)

formed once in four years and marched to the temple of the
goddess to present a costly robe for her statue. There was

ERECHTHEUM, RESTORED

color, too, about the temple,
blue and red and yellow, and
also gold; but the tints were
delicate and were used with
the most perfect skill. This
temple was built nearly twenty-
four hundred years ago. Hundreds of handsome structures
have been reared since then;
but even in the ruins of the Parthenon artists are constantly
discovering some new beauty. They find, for instance, that in
many places where later builders have used straight lines, the

Parthenon has curves. They find that, if the columns had been a little thicker or a little higher, they would not have seemed

so perfect. They find that the outer columns are not quite perpendicular, but slant inward. No one could discover this without the most careful measurements; but the slant, small as it is, helped to make the temple so graceful and firm and harmonious that, when it was completed, it looked as if it was the one building in all the world that had a right to be in that place.

The other buildings on the Acropolis were worthy to stand near the Parthenon. There was

A CARYATID
(From the Erechtheum)

the Er-ech-the'um, sacred to Athene and Poseidon, and within its bounds the sacred olive tree and the salt spring were still to be seen. There were wide marble steps leading up to the Acropolis; there were porticoes and colonnades; and there were porches whose roofs were upheld by strong and graceful car-y-at'-ids. Out under the clear blue sky stood another statue of Athene even larger than the one in the Parthenon. This was made of the Persian bronze captured at Marathon.

The artist to whom the glory of

THE DISCUS-THROWER
(From the statue by Myron)

the Acropolis is due was Phid'i-as. Before him sculptors had made lifelike statues of people; My'ron, for instance, had made a discus-thrower so true to life that one almost wonders why the discus does not fly from his hand; but artists had felt that statues of gods ought not to be very different from the stiff, formal figures that had represented them in earlier times. Phidias broke away from this notion. He made his gods like human

beings, but more grand and majestic than any person. One of his most famous works was the Zeus of Olympia, so wonderful a statue that when a man died who had never been to Olympia, the Greeks used to say, "That man was truly unfortunate, for he died without seeing the Olympian Zeus." Phidias was so anxious to do his best that, when people came to see his work, he used to stand just out of sight and listen to every word that even the humblest of them might say in criticism. Then, whenever he thought any one had discovered a fault, however small, he did not rest until he had corrected it.

THE OLYMPIAN ZEUS

Pericles also built the O-de'um, a great music hall, and he improved the theatre of Di-o-ny'sus. In Greece, a theatre was not a covered building. It consisted of rows upon rows of stone seats rising up the side of a hill, and circling about a level space where the plays were acted. A theatre was generally large enough to hold all the people of the city in which it stood. Some

THEATRE OF DIONYSUS, RESTORED

of the plays presented stories of the lives of the gods or noble deeds of the early Greeks. These were called tragedies. They were usually serious and dignified and sad, but often they con-

Tragedy and comedy

tained tender and beautiful verses. People came away from such plays feeling more inclined to honor the gods, or to be as brave and patriotic as their forefathers. Comedies were also acted. They were light and merry, and often full of jests about the men and actions of the day. The tragedies were so good teachers of religion and history and patriotism, and the comedies were of such value in setting people to thinking about what was going on around them, that Pericles wished even the poorest citizens to see them. Therefore it was ordered that the state should pay the admittance fee.

Plays were acted only twice a year; but at each festival there

were enough of them to make up for the six months' waiting.
Three poets were allowed to present four plays each. After the
plays had all been acted, a committee chosen by the demes
voted to which poet the state prize should be given. Thirteen
times it was voted to a man who was soldier as well as writer,
and had fought bravely at Marathon and Salamis and Platæa.
This was the poet Æs'chy-lus. His tragedies were exceedingly
fine, but so grave and serious that, after some years, the people
became a little tired of them and voted the prize to a handsome

Æschylus, sixth and fifth centuries B. C.

young poet named Soph'o-
cles, because his characters
were not quite so serious and
formal, and seemed more like
real people. He could not only
write plays but recite them,
and this talent stood him in
good stead in his old age. One
of his sons became alarmed
lest the father should give
away his property to a favorite grandchild. The great
dramatist was called into
court, that the judges might
see whether his intellect was
so enfeebled that he did not
realize what he was doing.

Sophocles, fifth century B. C.

THE THEATRE AT EPIDAURUS
(As the ruins appear to-day)

Instead of making any reply, Sophocles recited a passage from
one of his plays; and he did it so nobly that no one could fancy
him weak in mind. The judges rebuked the greedy son and sent
him away. The third great tragic poet was Eu-rip'i-des. He is

Euripides, fifth century B. C.

AESCHYLUS
(In the Capitol at Rome)

said to have taken his name from the battle of the Euripus, which was fought not long before he was born. He seemed to understand people even better than Sophocles, and he loved nature. It gave him real pleasure to write about the ocean, the rivers, clouds, rocks, vines, and birds.

The greatest writer of comedy was Ar-is-toph'a-nes, who lived a little later than these three tragic poets. He liked to make fun of his fellow citizens, and his fun was so keen and witty that the Athenians themselves could not help being amused by it. In one of his plays, "The Birds," two Athenians who are tired of the many lawsuits in their city flee from men to the birds and persuade them to build a city in the clouds. This was great sport for the Athenians, for nothing else seemed to them so entertaining as to go to court and listen to lawsuits. They must have laughed heartily when one of the characters said, —

"The Birds"

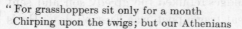

"For grasshoppers sit only for a month
  Chirping upon the twigs; but our Athenians

SOPHOCLES
(In the Lateran Museum at Rome)

Sit chirping and discussing all the year,
Perched upon points of evidence and law."

The "city in the clouds" was another jest at the expense of the Athenians, for only two years before that time they had sent out a military expedition which was a decided failure.

There were also two fine old historians who lived in the time of Pericles, He-rod'o-tus and Thu-cyd'i-des. It is Herodotus who tells us most of what we know about the Persian War. The world was a small place in those days when civilized men had seen so little of it, and Herodotus roamed over much of what was then known. Wherever he went, he kept his eyes open and he asked questions. Then he wrote what he had seen and heard. He writes as if he were telling a story. For instance, when he describes the passing of Xerxes over the Hellespont, he stops to tell what sort of caps or helmets the different nations had, and what kind of weapons they carried — all the little things that help to make a book interesting. He lingers over every point, as if he enjoyed telling the tale and was sure that his readers would like to hear it.

HERODOTUS AND THUCYDIDES
(From a double bust in the museum at Naples)

Herodotus, fifth century B. C.

The historian of the Persian War

There is a tradition — so good that it ought to be true — that he read his history at the Olympic games; that among the

Thucydides,
fifth century
B. C.
hearers was a boy of fifteen named Thucydides; and that when the boy heard the repeated shouts of applause, the tears came into his eyes and he said to himself, "I, too, will be a historian."

ANCIENT HELMETS

Thucydides became a historian as famous as Herodotus. He does not make his readers feel as if in telling a story he found quite so much pleasure as Herodotus; but he is so clear and fair, and sees so well the reasons for the events that he narrates, and states them so plainly and interestingly, that many later writers have read his works over and over, trying to learn to write as he wrote.

Thus it was that the Athenians flourished in the days of Pericles. They had slaves who did the hard work, and so left their masters time to enjoy poetry and art and **Prosperity of Athens** their beautiful city. There was little poverty, for to rear all these handsome new buildings there must be men who could work in wood, stone, brass, gold, and ivory, and who knew how to use dyes. There was plenty of work at good wages for the common laborers, and there was always need of embroiderers and painters and artists of all kinds. Then, too, the Atheni-

BRONZE LAMP IN THE FORM OF A BOAT
(Found in 1862 on the Acropolis at Athens)

ans knew how to make all sorts of earthenware and lamps, and indeed metal-work of many varieties. Captains and sailors were needed for the vessels that carried these to foreign lands and brought back loads of wine, glass, skins, salt fish, spices, dates, papyrus, carpets, gold, and slaves. Athens received every

year large sums of money from the members of the Delian League.
The other states declared that it was not fair for Athens to use
this money for her own purposes, and some of the Athenians
were of the same opinion; they said that Pericles had disgraced
the city by taking possession of the Delian treasury. Pericles

A GRECIAN HOME

and his party replied that the other members of the League had
given the money that they might be protected from the Persians
and from pirates, and that since Athens protected them, it was
only right for her to have the money and adorn the city with
buildings and statues that would be a glory to the state forever.
The opponents of Pericles retorted that there was now small

danger from pirates or Persians; but no money was returned, and the allies were still treated as subjects. The Athenians loved their city, and were so proud of her being the most beautiful city in Greece, that perhaps even those who differed from Pericles in this did not oppose him as they might otherwise have done.

Much as the Athenians liked magnificent temples, they were satisfied to live in plain, simple, flat-roofed houses. They spent so much time out of doors that a house was to them only a safe place for their family and their property and a shelter from storm. The side of the house that faced the street had some windows in the second story, but in the

CHAIR, COUCH, AND STOOL

The Athenian home

first there was only a small door. Here people knocked when they wished to go in; and they also knocked when they were ready to come out, for the doors swung outward, and were so heavy that a passer-by might easily be injured if struck by one of them. A slave sat in the narrow hall, ready to open the door. At the other end of the hall was a court with a colonnade around it. The rooms of the house opened into this court. They were not often large, and they did not contain expensive furniture. The chairs and couches and stools were all well-formed and pretty, but not costly. The beds were mattresses of wool stretched on straps or girths. There were many kinds of bowls and jars and cups, but all were of pleasing shapes; and the lamps especially were exceedingly graceful and elegant.

The clothes of the Greeks were as simple as the houses. The Athenian gentleman wore a long shirt, or *chiton*, of woolen or linen, and over this was thrown a nearly square cloak. The cloak was generally white, but sometimes colors were worn. It must be draped in precisely the correct way, for a man who wore his cloak draped from right to left instead of from left to right was sure to be laughed at. The Greeks saw no need of hats or caps unless it rained or they were obliged to make a journey in the hot sunshine. The Greek gentleman wore sandals, or, if he preferred, he went barefooted, but he must be sure not to forget his walking stick and his seal ring. The Athenian lady wore a *chiton* with sleeves, and over it a long loose robe fastened with a girdle. She had rings, not only on her fingers, but often in her ears and on her ankles. Little girls wore long dresses, but small boys were not much troubled with clothes of any sort unless the weather was cold.

WOMAN FASTENING HER ROBE WITH A GIRDLE

The dress of the Greeks

For food the Greeks had beef, lamb, pork, geese, ducks, and fish. They were especially fond of thrushes, and never ceased to be indignant with the dealers who blew air into the bodies of the birds to make them appear more plump. There were many kinds of vegetables and fruit. There was no sugar, but honey took its place so well that the Attic cooks were famous for their cakes. Much wine was used, but, just as in the days of Homer, the Greeks of the age of Pericles thought it greedy and vulgar to drink wine unmixed with water.

Their food

In the hearts of these busy Greeks there was a warm place for the children, and they were carefully watched and trained. They had as good a time playing as the boys and girls of to-day, and they played many of the same games. The girls had dolls made

The children

of wax or clay, and the boys had tops and iron hoops and hobby-horses and carts and kites. There were stilts and swings and see-saws, there were different games of ball, and there were tag and blind-man's-buff. Until the children were about seven years old, the boys and girls played together and were treated much alike; but after that time matters became quite different, for now the boys must go to school. So while the little girl stayed at home and learned of her mother to read and write and care for a house, the boy was put into the care of a slave, called a pedagogue, who took him to school, brought him home, carried his tablets, and saw

BOY WITH CART AND DOG
(From an Athenian vase-painting)

that he behaved well on the street and kept out of mischief. The boy learned the alphabet and then he learned to read. No slipshod reading was allowed. Every word must ring clear and true, and every thought must be brought out properly before the master was satisfied. The boy learned to write on a tablet covered with wax. He drew the letters with a little pointed instrument of metal or bone called a stylus; then the wax was smoothed and made ready for him to follow another copy. After he had learned to write, he had to write whatever the mas-

Greek boys at school

GREEK BOY'S HANDWRITING FOUND
ON THE WALLS OF A GREEK HOUSE

ter read. These dictations were not simple stories for children; they were selections from the Iliad or the Odyssey, some of the proverbs of Hesiod, or some graceful lyric of Pindar or Simonides. The boy need not write rapidly, but he must write clearly and well, for on the following day the master would call upon him to read what he had written. Finally, he was obliged to learn Subjects taught it by heart. He was also taught to reckon, to sing, to play on the lyre, and perhaps to draw. He learned to dance, to run, to leap, to wrestle, and to throw the javelin and the discus. It was not probable that many of the boys would ever gain an Olympian prize, but every one was expected to make his body strong and to learn how to use his muscles. A boy might not be able to win a foot-race, but he could learn to carry himself well and to run with such ease that it was a pleasure to watch him.

This was the teaching of young boys which the Greeks of the noblest years of Greece believed would train them to become good men and good citizens. When the boy was eighteen or nineteen years old, he became a citizen. His name was enrolled as a member of a deme. A sword and a shield were given him, and he

LESSON IN MUSIC AND GRAMMAR IN AN ATHENIAN SCHOOL

(From a cup-painting. At the right is the pedagogue)

was called upon to take a solemn oath to honor religion, to fight for his country, and to strive to leave it better than he found it.

The age of Pericles, or that part of it during which Greece was at the height of her glory, is counted as lasting only from The Age of Pericles 445 B. C. to 431 B. C. because, although it had been agreed that the treaty should last for thirty years, it was only fifteen before it was broken. During those fifteen years there was peace in the land of the Greeks, in Persia, Spain, Italy, Gaul, in all the countries that were then known. The one exception was the revolt of two members of the Delian League, Byzantium and Samos; but Pericles succeeded in crushing these rebellions. Those fifteen years were the proudest time in the history of Athens. The city was rich and strong and beautiful and happy; and yet in only a few short years, the Athenians had become so wretched and miserable as narrowly to escape being sold as slaves.

TWO VIEWS OF A GREEK CHILD'S HEAD

SUMMARY

Pericles brought it about that all who held office or worked for the state should be paid. Among these were several thousand jurors.

Pericles planned a wonderful group of buildings and statues on the Acropolis. The noblest was the Parthenon.

Phidias made statues of the gods like human beings, but more grand and majestic.

Pericles also built the Odeum, and adorned the theatre of Dionysus.

Tragedies made the people wish to honor the gods and be brave and patriotic. Comedies made them think about public events. The state paid the admittance fees that all might see the plays.

Æschylus took the state prize for the best play thirteen times: then it fell to Sophocles. A third tragic poet was Euripides. Aristophanes was the greatest writer of comedy.

Herodotus and Thucydides were famous historians.

Athens was now rich and prosperous. Much money came to her from the Delian League.

The Athenians lived in simple houses and wore simple clothes. They had a variety of food. Honey took the place of sugar.

Children played many of the games of to-day. They were carefully trained. The little girl was taught by her mother; the boy went to school.

The Age of Pericles lasted from 445 B. C. to 431 B. C. It was the proudest time in the history of Athens.

SUGGESTIONS FOR WRITTEN WORK

A visit to the Acropolis.

A visit to an Athenian home.

A Greek boy describes a day at school.

XIV

THE STRUGGLE BETWEEN ATHENS AND SPARTA, OR THE PELOPONNESIAN WAR

WHILE Athens had been growing rich and strong and beautiful, Sparta had kept to her old rough way of living. She had no stately buildings, no statues, no exquisite carvings, no elaborate embroideries. To think that a people who cared for such foolish things should claim the leadership of Greece made the Spartans more and more scornful of their rivals. They had agreed to keep the peace for thirty years, but they were not sorry when an act of the Athenians gave them an excuse for breaking it.

The Spartans break the peace

The fighting did not begin in either Athens or Sparta, but far away in the Ionian Sea, near the island of Cor-cy′ra. Trouble had arisen between Corcyra and the mother city, Corinth, and in a naval battle the island had won the victory. When the Cor-cy-re'ans saw how many ships Corinth was building, they became frightened and asked to join the Athenian league. What

The Athenians favor Corcyra

reply the Athenians should give was a serious matter. "The Peace of Pericles permits a city not already belonging to any league to join either the Athenian or the Peloponnesian," urged the Corcyreans. "But not with the express purpose of injuring a

THE WESTERN COAST OF CORCYRA

member of the other," retorted the Corinthians. The Athenians were in a hard position. They realized that sooner or later there would be war between themselves and the Spartans. Corinth was an ally of Sparta, and if she overcame the Corcyreans and added their fleet to her own, she would be altogether too strong on the water to please the Athenians.

Then, too, Corcyra was a valuable ally, not only because she had a large fleet, but because the island was a convenient stopping-place on the way to Italy, and because, if the Spartans should ever attack the western coast, it would be worth a great deal to have a friend so near. The Athenians could not make up their minds either to lose those ships and the friendship of the island or to break the treaty boldly. They finally settled matters in a half-way fashion by agreeing to send ten ships into the Ionian

They break the treaty with Sparta

Sea, "not to fight with the Corinthians, but to protect Corcyra," they said. When a second naval battle took place between Corcyra and Corinth, the Athenians tried at first only to hinder the Corinthian ships without actually attacking them; but when the Corcyreans began to get the worst of it and started to retreat, the Athenians forgot all about the Peace of Pericles and fought as fiercely as if they had never heard of such a thing.

Sparta and the other Peloponnesian states were indignant, and soon they held a sort of court to try the city of Athens. Several cities told how unjustly Athens had treated them. They said that she was dishonorable and was constantly trying to get control of more states. Some Athenian envoys happened to be in Sparta on other business, and they asked if they might speak to the assembly. They reviewed what Athens had done in the Persian War, and showed that she had really been the savior of all Greece. "Our allies came of their own accord," declared the envoys, "and asked us to be their leaders and protectors. An empire was offered us; can you wonder that we accepted it and refused to give it up again?" After the envoys and strangers had gone, the Spartans discussed matters. They decided that the Athenians had broken the treaty. Then both countries began to make ready for war.

Pericles knew that the Spartans would ravage Attica; therefore he persuaded the Attic farmers to come within the city walls. Then were seen long lines of sorrowful men, women, and children slowly making their way to Athens. Their backs were bowed with heavy burdens, for they knew well that whatever was left would be destroyed. From the Acropolis they could see their homes and the fields of ripening grain. A little later they saw the smoke rising from the burning houses, they saw the grain-fields cut down and ruined by the Spartans. It is small wonder that they cried out, "O Pericles, lead us out to battle; lead us out as a general should!" But Pericles said "No." "The Spartans are strong on

The congress to try Athens

The Attic farmers flee to Athens

the land," he had declared long before, "but our strength is on the sea." Therefore he had sent ships to cruise around the Peloponnesus, doing all the damage possible, but he would not go out to meet the enemy in a land battle. After ravaging the fields, the Spartans went home. They might as well have tried to fly to the moon as to break through the mighty walls of Athens. Another season, however, they had a helper not on their list of allies, for the plague appeared in the crowded city, and multitudes died. It came again; and now Athens lost the one man

Death of Pericles

who might have saved her, for soon Pericles lay dying. His friends sat about his bed, sorrowing and speaking together of his victories. Suddenly the dying man opened his eyes and said, "You dwell upon these acts of mine, though many other generals have performed the like; but you take no notice of the most honorable part of my character, that no Athenian through my means ever put on mourning."

The revolt of Mytilene, 428–427 B. C.

Now came the time when Athens might well have wished that her allies were her friends, for news came to her that Myt-i-le′ne, a city on the island of Lesbos, had revolted. Mytilene had a large fleet, therefore her loss would be of much importance. Athenian forces were sent at once to besiege the city, the Spartan ships that had been promised were slow in coming to her aid, and finally Mytilene was forced to yield. She had surrendered to a cruel master, for the Athenians were not only indignant at the revolt, but also much alarmed lest there should be other revolts. With hardly a moment's thought they decreed that every man in Mytilene should be put to death and every woman and child sold as a slave. If Pericles had been alive, no such inhuman decree would have been passed, but the Athenians were now much

Cleon

influenced by a man named Cle′on. "Do not be merciful to them," he said; "punish them as they would have punished you. Be forgiving and virtuous if you like, but wait till forgiveness and virtue are no longer dangerous." The decree was passed, though the better part of the Athenians were so ashamed of it that the following morning they called another meeting and annulled it. But the trireme that carried the decree had sailed the previous night. Would it be possible to overtake it? "We will provide wine and barley for the crew," the envoys of the Myt-i-le-ne'ans

The decree of death passed

ATHENIAN TRIREME
(From a bas-relief found on the Acropolis at Athens)

cried eagerly, "and every man shall have a generous reward if they reach the island first." The rowers sprang to their seats. Half of them rowed by day and half by night, and they ate their barley, kneaded with wine and oil, as they rowed. Nevertheless, the first vessel had too long a start. The decree had been read aloud, and the order to carry it out at once was on the point of being given when the second vessel touched the land. An envoy rushed up the shore to the commander, and the Athenians were saved from the shame of such a barbarous slaughter. The punishment that they did inflict was terrible enough, for they put to

The decree revoked

death one thousand of those who had been most prominent among the rebels, took away the ships of the Mytileneans, and gave their land to Athenian citizens for a settlement.

Such was the mercy of the Athenians. That same year the mercy of the Spartans was shown at Platæa. They had set out to conquer Platæa because the little city was so faithful a friend to Athens. "But the Spartans together with the other states took a solemn oath that our city should be forever independent," declared the Platæans. "What you say is just," returned the Spartans. "Enjoy your independence, but help us to free the states that are now ruled by Athens." Platæa, however, would not desert the Athenians, and the siege began. Thucydides wrote the history of the Peloponnesian War, and in it is an account of this siege written in his usual clear, accurate, interesting fashion. First, the Spartans cut down trees and made a palisade around the city, so that no one could get in or out. They wanted a mound high enough to enable them to shoot down into the city, and they began to make one near the wall by piling up logs crosswise and filling the empty spaces with stones and earth and pieces of wood. Night and day they worked for ten long weeks. Somehow the mound did not grow as fast as they thought it should, and at length they discovered that the Platæans had made a hole at the base of the wall and were quietly drawing the loose earth from the mound into the city. Meanwhile, they were also making the wall higher by building it up with brick and timber from their houses. The Spartans could have set this work afire with burning arrows, but the Platæans were wise enough to keep heavy curtains of hides and skins in front of it. The besiegers were determined that there should be no more stealing from their mound, and so instead of filling it in with loose dirt, they now used masses

The siege
of Platæa,
429–427
B. C.

The able defense of the
Platæans

of clay and reeds bound together.
Still the mound did not grow. What
could be the matter, they wondered.
Finally, some one discovered that
those wily Platæans had dug a tun-
nel from the city to the mound, and
were drawing in the bundles of clay
and reeds at their leisure. This was
not all, for they were building an
inner wall in the shape of a crescent.
The horns touched the outer wall,
and the curve was toward the city.
If the Spartans should take the outer
wall, they would still have the crescent to capture, and this would not
be easy with the Platæans in front

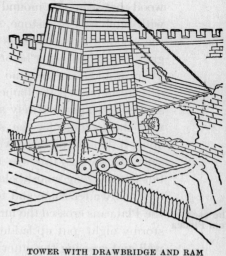

TOWER WITH DRAWBRIDGE AND RAM
(Used in attacking a walled city)

and on both sides of them. The Spartans thought of that, of
course, and they brought up immense battering-rams; but the
Platæans had two ways of managing rams. One way was to drop
a noose over them and draw them up. The other was to hang
heavy beams directly over them and at right angles to them.

A HAND RAM

When the engine was in good
position and ready to give a
tremendous blow upon the
wall, down went the beam,
and off went the head of the
ram. Then the Spartans decided to burn the city. They
threw quantities of wood over
the wall and piled masses of

The Spar-
tans decide
to burn
Platæa

wood between the mound and the wall. They daubed sticks with pitch and brimstone, set them afire, and hurled them after the wood. Such a blaze as there was! Thucydides says that so great a fire had never before been made by the hands of man. There would have been no help for the Platæans had not a sudden storm put out the flames. Then the Spartans built two walls sixteen feet apart entirely around the city. Between these walls were the lodgings for the soldiers; so that, when the work was done, it looked like one very thick wall with a moat on either side. As soon as this was finished, the main army went away, but left a strong guard behind.

The escape from Platæa

When winter came and food began to be scanty, a number of the Platæans crossed the inner moat, full of broken ice, one dark, stormy night, put up ladders, and succeeded in getting over the wall and crossing the outer moat. "The Spartans will expect us to try to get to Athens," they said, "so let us start in the direction of Thebes." As they glanced hurriedly back through the darkness, toward the road to Athens, they could see the torches of their pursuers. After a while the fugitives slipped away to the hills and down narrow paths, and soon they were being welcomed at Athens by the women and children who had been sent there before the siege began.

Pitiful condition of those remaining

Within the walls of Platæa there were now some women-servants and two hundred and twenty-five men, too weak for want of food to be able to defend their city longer. The Spartans could have taken it by storm, but when the war closed, places taken by storm would probably be given back to their former rulers, while those that had surrendered would be kept by the victors. "Will you surrender if we promise you a fair trial?" the Spartans asked, and the famished people yielded. The Thebans hated the Platæans, and the Spartans wished to please the Thebans; therefore the "fair trial" consisted chiefly of the question, "Have you done any service for the Spartans or their allies in this war?" As each Platæan answered "No," he was led away and put to death. Every man in Platæa was slain, and the serving-women were sold as slaves. Such was the mercy of the Spartans.

A war between men of the same race is always more bitter than other wars, because each side feels that the others *must* know **Bitterness of the war** themselves to be in the wrong: and this war became more and more savage. In almost every city there were two parties,—one that thought the people as a whole ought to rule, as in Athens; the other that thought the government

PYLOS

should be in the hands of a few, as in Sparta. These parties quarreled and fought. Sons killed their fathers, and fathers killed their sons. If two men were enemies, one or the other was sure to become a murderer. If a man owed money, he freed himself from his debt by killing his creditor. The whole Grecian world seemed to have gone mad, not only the mainland of Greece, but the **The war spreads to colonies and islands** islands, and even the colonies of Italy and Sicily. The two parties within each city tried to slaughter each other; cities fought against cities; Athenian ships swept across the sea to help some town, and Spartan ships made all speed to help its enemy. There was fighting on the land and on the sea for six long years.

In the seventh year an Athenian fleet was storm-bound in the harbor of Py'los on the Messenian coast. This fell in perfectly with the wishes of the general, De-mos'the-nes,[1] for he had a plan to propose to the other officers. "Let us fortify this place," he said. "We are but forty-six miles from Sparta; the Messenians will help us; and from here we can do great damage to the enemy." The other officers scorned the plan. "If you want to waste the public money," they said, "there are plenty of other desolate promontories that you can fortify." The storm-wind still blew, and the ships could not leave the harbor. It may be that the soldiers were bored and restless with the long stay; but whatever the reason was, permission was at length given them to build the fort. They had no tools to shape the stones, so they fitted them together as best they could. They had nothing in which to carry the mortar, so they heaped it up on their backs and clasped their hands behind them to keep it from falling off; and the fort was built.

Building a
fort at Pylos,
425 B. C.

PYLOS AND SPHACTERIA

When the Spartans heard of this rather remarkable structure, they laughed. "It will be easy enough to tear that down any time," they said, "even if the Athenians do not run when they see us coming." However, they concluded it was best to get rid of the fort at once, and also of the Athenian ships left on guard; so they sent a fleet and a goodly

The struggle at Pylos number of soldiers. The soldiers were landed on a long, narrow island called Sphac-te'ri-a, which almost shut in the harbor of

---

[1] Not the **orator** Demosthenes.

Pylos. The Spartan ships sailed into the harbor and tried for two days to take the rough little fort. Then came the Athenian fleet sweeping down upon them, for they had delayed to close up the harbor. The Spartans on shore were frantic, for their friends on Sphacteria were helpless. They dashed into the water, armed as they were, and tried to pull their empty ships away from the Athenians. Thucydides says the Spartans were carrying on a sea fight from the land, and the Athenians were waging a land fight from their ships.

The Spartans are overcome and sue for peace

So many of their prominent men were on the island that the Spartans decided to ask the Athenians to make peace. The Athenians would probably have agreed if it had not been for Cleon. After the death of Pericles, Cleon had done everything that he could to please the people and keep them from following the advice of wiser men. He now persuaded the Athenians to refuse peace ex-

GREEK BOAT SCULPTURED IN ROCK

cept on terms that he knew the Spartans would not accept. He did this because he thought there was a better chance for him to rise in war than in peace.

The Athenians were always fickle and changeable, and soon they turned upon Cleon. "Why did you keep us from making peace?" they demanded. "Our men at Pylos will starve. We can hardly get food to them now, and when winter comes they will surely have to surrender. The Spartan soldiers on the island are safe and comfortable. The Spartans pay a great price to every man who will run the blockade and carry them food. If the man is a Helot, one little voyage makes him free. Hundreds of Helots

The Athenians blame Cleon

dive and swim across, and drag after them skins of pounded lin-
seed and poppy-seed mixed with honey. Whenever there is a
strong on-shore wind, hundreds more sail out to sea in the night,
and with the first light they dash up on the ocean side of the
island. The Spartans on Sphacteria have plenty of meal and wine
and cheese, while the Athenians at Pylos are starving. It is your
fault; why did you refuse to make peace?"

Cleon could think of nothing else to do than to grumble at the
generals. "They could easily sail to Sphacteria and capture the
Spartan soldiers," he declared. "That is what I would do if I were
commander." One of the generals, Nic′i-as, was present. "So
far as the generals are concerned, you may take whatever force
you wish and try it. Here in the presence of the assembly, I
resign to you the command." "Take it, take it," shouted the
multitude; "we make you general. Now sail for Pylos." The
fickle Athenians had forgotten all about the sufferings of their
soldiers, and they were greatly amused to see the dismay of Cleon.
He knew that he must either slink away or accept the command.
He screwed up his courage and turned upon them. "I am not
afraid of the Spartans," he retorted. "Within twenty days I will
kill them on the spot or else bring them to you alive." The
rabble burst into shouts of laughter, and the wiser folk were as
pleased as the rabble were amused. "We have seen the last of
Cleon," they said, "unless he really should capture the Spartans."

No one expected the boaster to have any success, but within
twenty days he actually did bring back to Athens nearly three
hundred prisoners. This is the way it came about. When Cleon
reached the island of Sphacteria, he found that the forest which
had covered most of it had been burned. The country was cleared,
and the general in command was about to make an attack upon

*Cleon be-
comes com-
mander*

*The capture
of Sphac-
teria*

the prisoners. Cleon had no plan, so he fell in with this one. There was a hard fight, but finally the Spartans lowered their shields and waved their hands; they had yielded. Then all Greece was amazed. Could this be the same race that had fought at Thermopylæ until the last man fell? The Athenians could hardly believe the surrender was possible. They were jubilant over their victory, and when the Spartans again asked peace, they refused.

So the war continued, and on both sides men grew more savage and brutal. The nobles at Corcyra favored Sparta and conspired against the common folk, who favored Athens. Through a trick the nobles were captured and put to death with horrible cruelty. **The Corcyrean nobles put to death** Thus far the Athenians had on the whole been the winning party. They had tried to take De'li-um in Bœotia and had failed; but they held Pylos, which was the key to Messenia; and Cy-the'ra, which had been a great protection to Laconia; and one hundred of the prominent Spartans were their prisoners. The Spartans had made a raid into Attica once a year and had done considerable fighting elsewhere, but they were not one step nearer conquering the Athenians than they had been seven years before. Fortunately for them, a new general appeared on the scene, Bras'i-das. He was as deter-

SAILING VESSEL OF THE TIME OF BRASIDAS

mined as any Spartan and as bright and quick as any Athenian. He thought the matter over. "If we make another raid into Attica, the Athenians will put our hundred citizens to death. **Brasidas takes command of Spartans** The best thing we can do is to strike at Thrace — and we shall be sure of a welcome from more than one Thracian city. Thrace is rich and has widespreading forests. With her for a friend we can build ships, and then we need have no fear of meeting the Athenians on the water."

So said Brasidas. The Spartans thought this was a wild, unreasonable plan; but there was one thing strongly in its favor, — Brasidas had about one thousand men whom he had hired in different parts of the Peloponnesus, and all that he asked of Sparta was to give him seven hundred Helots. "Let him try it," said the Spartans. "The Helots are on the point of revolting, and it will be a good thing to get some of them out of the way. He may take a city or two, and when the war is over we can exchange them for Pylos."

The plan of Brasidas

So Brasidas started for Thrace and Macedonia. He was not only a keen, shrewd man, but he also knew how to talk and argue and persuade. He even induced tribes friendly to the Athenians to allow him to pass through their lands; and he half-persuaded and half-threatened several cities in Thrace and Chal-cid'i-ce to yield to him. The Athenians had heard what he was doing, and now they came down upon him. Cleon was their leader, and he was so elated because of the victory at Pylos, that he expected to win as a matter of course. He had good soldiers, but they did not believe in their general. Nearly half of Brasidas's men were Helots, but they had a leader whom they could trust, and, slaves as they were, he was not afraid to trust them. Just before the attack upon Am-phip'o-lis, the strongest Athenian colony in Macedonia, he told them how he planned to carry it on. His last words to them were, "Do not lose heart; think of all that is at stake; and I will show you that I can not only advise others, but can myself fight." The battle ended in a victory for the Spartans. Both Cleon and Brasidas were slain. Thucydides was in command of seven

BRONZE COIN SHOWING SHIP UNDER SAIL

(On deck the pilot and oarsmen can be seen)

The Spartans victorious

ships not far away, but he did not arrive soon enough to prevent the Spartans from winning. The Athenians wanted to blame some one, and they fixed upon him. He was exiled for twenty years. Then it was that he wrote his history of the war. The Helots who had fought so bravely with Brasidas were made free.

There had now been ten years of warfare. Men had been slain, women and children sold into slavery, money wasted, fleets lost, lands ravaged, cities destroyed; and what gain had come of it? The Spartans had discovered that it was quite possible for them to be beaten, or, what the men of Thermopylæ would have thought far worse, to be forced into a surrender; the Athenians had learned that in spite of their fleet, their sheltered harbor, and their mighty walls, they would be little stronger than other people if their tributary cities should revolt. Both Spartans and Athenians were sobered and were ready to talk of peace. The general Nicias had much to do with arranging it, and therefore the truce of fifty years which was agreed upon in 421 B. C. is called the Peace of Nicias.

SUMMARY

The Athenians broke the Peace of Pericles.

The Attic farmers fled to Athens, and the Spartans ravaged Attica. Many Athenians died of the plague.

Mytilene revolted against Athens.

The Spartans conquered Platæa. The war became more and more bitter.

The Athenians built a fort at Pylos. The Spartans failed to take the fort. The Athenians refused to make peace, and the Spartans surrendered.

Thus far the Athenians had been the winning party.

The Spartan Brasidas was successful in Thrace and Macedonia.

The Peace of Nicias was signed in 421 B. C.

SUGGESTIONS FOR WRITTEN WORK

A Spartan tells why Sparta will surely conquer Athens.

A Platæan describes the siege of Platæa.

An Athenian soldier describes the building of the fort at Pylos.

XV

THE SICILIAN EXPEDITION

Many leagues and alliances

THE chief good accomplished by the Peace of Nicias was to stop the fighting for two or three years. During this time so many leagues and alliances were formed among the Greeks that it is a wonder how any state could make sure who were her friends and who were her enemies. The allies of Sparta were indignant because, as they claimed, she had done well for herself in the treaty, but had taken no care of their interests. Many of the captured towns objected to being given back to their former rulers, as the treaty required. Then Athens and Sparta made a private agreement to force their allies to obey the treaty. The state of Ar'go-lis had kept neutral during the war and had spent the time in growing rich and strong. Argolis now made a league with some of Sparta's dissatisfied allies; and to cap the climax, Athens joined this league also. Sparta saw that unless the Ar-gol'ic league was broken, she would lose her power in the Peloponnesus, so she attacked the Ar-go'li-ans, who were aided by the Athenians. A battle was fought at Man-ti-ne'a, and the Spartans won such a victory that Argolis gave up all hope of ever leading the Peloponnesus.

Mantinea, 418 B. C.

Meanwhile the Athenians had fixed their eyes upon Me'los, one of the two islands in the Ægean Sea that they did not rule. They sent a fleet against it and ordered the Me'li-ans to yield or lose their city. "We are Dorians, and surely the Spartans will come to help us," thought the Melians; but no help came. The city The Athenians capture Melos fell. All the grown men were put to death, and the women and children sold as slaves. Such barbarity was nothing new in those days, but there had been no reason for attacking the island except that Athens wanted it, and Greece was horrified at the deed.

MELOS

The Athenians, however, were thinking of nothing but how to make their empire larger. They seemed to feel that if they owned a great deal of land or could oblige many cities to pay them tribute, they must be powerful. They ruled the islands to the east of Greece, — why should they not go west and conquer the wealthy They plan to conquer Sicily island of Sicily? To be sure, they knew well that the Peloponnesian War was not over by any means, and that Pericles had said it would be ruinous for them to try to enlarge their empire while war was going on; but they had begun to think the ideas of Pericles were old-fashioned. The able general Nicias reminded his countrymen how many men they had lost by war and by the plague, and urged them not to send troops to Sicily, when with only a few days' warning every soldier might be needed at home. "An expedition to Sicily is a serious business," he declared, "and not one which a mere youth can plan and carry into execution off-hand." So said Nicias, but the Athenians were beginning to

Schopin

SOCRATES INSTRUCTING ALCIBIADES

call Nicias slow and cautious, and they paid no heed to his words.

Alcibiades

The "mere youth" was a young man named Al-ci-bi′a-des. He was rich, handsome, and of a noble family. He was the most eloquent speaker in Athens, and of so brilliant a mind that the wise and kindly philosopher Socrates became very fond of him and tried his best to keep him from being spoiled. This was not an easy thing to do, for there was something about Alcibiades that seemed to dazzle people and make them forget to be reasonable and sensible. He won the favor of the crowd by paying for the production of plays to amuse them, by keeping fast horses, by winning Olympian prizes in the chariot races, and by a certain daring and boldness that fascinated them. To almost every one but Socrates he was rude and impudent; and yet people usually forgave him. They would say, "Oh, it is only Alcibiades's way," and watch to see what his next prank would be. He once refused an invitation to a feast; but when the other guests were at table, he suddenly appeared at the door with his servants and swept away half of the golden dishes; but the host still remained his admiring friend. Alcibiades's wild companions "dared" him to commit all sorts of insolent acts. One was to walk up to one of the most dignified citizens of Athens and box his ears. This man disapproved of the young noble, and refused to look upon such boorishness as a merry jest; but early the next morning Alcibiades appeared at his door, threw off his trailing purple robe, and said, "I have come that you may beat me. Chastise me as you please"; and he was forgiven. If all his freaks had been merely as silly and impudent as these, he might perhaps have been pardoned; but in spite of all of Socrates's teaching, he was utterly dishonorable. The wiser people of Athens saw this; but the masses were pleased with any one who entertained them.

His wild deeds

Such was the leader whom the Athenians were ready to follow on the maddest expedition that a people ever undertook. Nicias spoke once more and told the assembly that the cities of Sicily were rich and had large numbers of troops. "If you decide to make this invasion," he said, "you must have at least one hundred triremes, a multitude of soldiers, a vast supply of food, and a great sum of money." He had hoped that they would not be so eager if they realized what immense preparations were needed; but, on the contrary, the excitable, hot-headed people were half beside themselves with delight because they were entering upon so prodigious an undertaking. They had perhaps lost a few cities in Thrace and Macedonia, but why should they trouble themselves to win them back when they would so soon be lords of a

Nicias opposes the Sicilian invasion

The Athenians dream of conquest

splendid new empire in the west? They would first overcome Sicily; but this was only a beginning, for they would then press on to the conquest of Italy and Africa. There would be adventures and wealth and glory for every one. It was a quest for the golden fleece, and they never doubted that they should slay the dragon.

Sicily had been settled by colonists from various countries. Few of those who came from Greece were Athenians, but there were many Dorians. Syracuse was founded by Corinthian Dorians, and it was now the largest and richest of the Greek cities ex-

GOING ON BOARD

cept Athens. The cities of Sicily had sometimes quarreled, and the Athenians had once sent a fleet to help a Eubœan city against Syracuse. The pretext for invading the island again was that a little town called E-ges'ta had asked Athens for help in her quarrel with Se-li'nus, another little town that was aided by Syracuse. "We are ready to pay all costs," declared the E-ges-tæ'ans, "if Athens will only help us with her fleet and forces." The Athenians did one sensible thing, they sent envoys to find out whether Egesta really had the wealth of which she boasted. When the envoys returned, they brought back with them money enough to pay the crews of sixty triremes for one month, and they had amazing stories to tell of the mag-

The borrowed silver and gold vessels

nificent silver bowls and flagons and other offerings that they had seen in the temples. "We were feasted again and again," they said, "and at every feast we were served from superb drinking-vessels of silver and gold." They had not been observing enough to wonder why all the Egestæans had precisely the same kind of dishes and ornaments, and it never entered their minds that those enterprising colonists had been borrowing of one another and of the neighboring cities in order to persuade the Athenians that they were exceedingly wealthy.

Great was the bustle of preparation. Food, arms, ships, money, troops, must all be made ready. In the midst of the cheerful confusion the Athenians awoke one morning and were horrified. Some one had gone through the city mutilating the Her'mæ, or heads of Hermes into which the stone posts were carved that stood at the doors of houses and temples. "It is a fearful insult to the gods, and they will avenge it upon us," whispered the Athenians in dismay. Then their dismay turned to anger. Who had done such a deed? They remembered that only one man had ever played such mad pranks as this. "It was surely Alcibiades," declared his enemies boldly. "He hoped for a revolution that should throw the government into the hands of the nobles." "Give me a fair trial," Alcibiades demanded; but his enemies urged that the expedition ought not to be delayed, and the ships sailed. The whole population of Athens flocked to the Piræus to see them off, for this was the most costly armament ever sent out by any state of Greece. There were men from every city that was subject to the Athenians. The ships were perfectly equipped, the crews were the best that could be found. The soldiers vied with one another in the excellence of their arms and accoutrements. When all was ready, the trumpet sounded for silence, and all those thousands stood hushed and motionless. Then a herald repeated a prayer to the gods; the whole fleet and the multitudes on the shore said it with him. On every ship, wine mingled with

The mutilation of the Hermæ

The sailing of the Sicilian expedition

water was poured out in sacrifice to the gods from bowls of silver or of gold. The crews sang a hymn in honor of Apollo. Then the ships put out to sea in single file, sailing and rowing rapidly toward Corcyra.

The three plans proposed

When they reached Rhe'gi-um, the Italian town nearest to Sicily, they landed and sent envoys to Egesta. Nicias had never believed in the vast wealth of the Egestæans, and now their falsehoods and boasting were revealed. The three generals consulted. "Let us oblige the Egestæans to pay what they promised, force Selinus to come to terms, and then go home," urged Nicias. "Let us attack Syracuse at once, before she can prepare for war,"

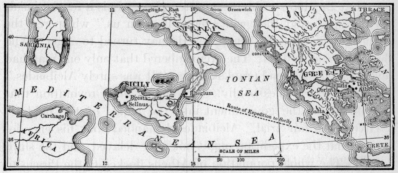

ROUTE OF THE EXPEDITION TO SICILY

advised Lam'a-chus. "Let us first gain as many allies in Sicily as we can and then attack Syracuse," counseled Alcibiades. This last plan was decided upon.

Alcibiades is called home

Suddenly a ship arrived from Athens with orders for Alcibiades to come home for the trial that had been refused him before the fleet set out. His enemies had delayed it until the troops were in Sicily, for they knew that so popular a commander would surely be acquitted if they were in Athens. He was now accused of another crime, ridiculing with some of his wild companions the holy El-eu-sin'i-an Mysteries. These were the most sacred and most secret of the religious rites of the Greeks; to reveal them or to mimic them was looked upon as a crime deserving death. Alcibiades had no idea of standing trial under such circumstances. He had been allowed to start for home in his own ship, guarded by the messenger vessel. It was not difficult for him to escape; and the messenger vessel had to return to Greece without him.

The serious charge against him

It was some months before the plan to lay siege to Syracuse was carried out, but both sides were busy. The Athenians sent home for money and cavalry

RUINS OF THE TEMPLE OF ELEUSIS
(Chief seat of the Eleusinian Mysteries)

and formed alliances with as many of the people of Sicily as possible. The Syr-a-cu'sans built new fortifications for the city and strengthened the old ones. They also sent envoys to Corinth and Sparta, asking for help and begging Sparta to renew the war against Athens, so that the Athenians would have to send for their soldiers. When these envoys reached Sparta, they met there an eloquent, fascinating young traitor who was all ready to make a speech to the Spartans in their behalf. It was Alcibiades himself. "I know the secrets of the Athenians," he declared. "I have lost an ungrateful country, but I have not lost the power of doing you service, if you will listen to me." There was no question about his hearers being attentive, for he

Alcibiades becomes a traitor

proceeded to tell the Spartans and the Syracusan envoys all about the Athenian plans for taking first Syracuse, then Carthage, and then attacking Sparta and her allies. "The safety, not of Sicily alone, but of the Peloponnesus is at stake," he declared, as earnestly as if he had been born a Spartan. Then he gave them some sound advice. In the first place, he urged them to send forces to Syracuse, and above all a skillful Spartan commander; then, to make war against Athens at once. "You ought to fortify Dec-e-le′a straightway," he said; "the Athenians are always in dread of this." He went on to explain to them that if the Spartans held Decelea, the Athenians would lose the usual tribute, the income from the land and from the silver mines; and as the place was only fourteen miles from Athens, there was no question that numbers of slaves would escape from Athens to Decelea. The Spartans concluded to follow his advice. They began to prepare their fleet and they took possession of Decelea.

His advice to the Spartans

In Sicily all was working so well for the Athenians that the Syracusans were on the point of arranging for a surrender. Suddenly a Corinthian ship appeared in their harbor. "Ships are coming from Sparta," said the commander. "Gy-lip′pus, the greatest Spartan general, is on his way to help you." Soon Gylippus appeared with ships and men. The Athenians were cheerfully building a wall around Syracuse, but that work had to stop abruptly, for Gylippus built a cross-wall. The Athenians sent more ships and another general, Demosthenes, who had built the fort at

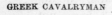

GREEK CAVALRYMAN

Pylos. They made attacks by sea and by land, but they did not take Syracuse. The Athenian camp was in an unhealthy place

and many of the soldiers were ill. "The city cannot be taken,"
declared Demosthenes. "Let us retreat while we are able."
The moon was full, but suddenly it went into eclipse. "What
does it signify?" Nicias demanded anxiously of the soothsayers.
"It signifies that for three times nine days the army must not
move," they replied. Nicias believed firmly in the soothsayers.
The army waited and lost its one chance of escape.

The Syracusans were no longer afraid of losing their city. Now
they were in quest of glory, and they planned to capture the
whole fleet of the invaders. Then followed a most terrible battle.
The Syracusan ships blocked the entrance of the harbor; the
Athenian triremes could not escape to the open sea. Two hundred
vessels were crowded into the narrow space. Ships were driven
against ships, sometimes two or three dashed into one. "Force
your way or never see Greece again!" cried the Athenian generals to their men. "Win the victory! Make your city glorious!"
shouted the Syracusan officers; but the creaking, the crashing,
the screeching, the groaning, the clanking of chains, the sound of
savage blows, and the heavy thud of men falling dead upon the
decks — these were so loud that only those nearest could hear
the words of their officers. Except for the troops on board the
two fleets, all Syracuse was on one part of the shore, and all the
Greeks on another. The Greeks pressed down to the water's
edge; they groaned and sobbed and shrieked in agony when one
of their vessels was disabled; they shouted with joy when one appeared for a moment to have escaped; they swayed to and fro;
they threw themselves on the ground; they stretched up their
arms in prayer to the gods. The Syracusan ships were here, there,
and everywhere. The Athenians rowed frantically toward the
entrance to the harbor; they were thrust back upon the shore;

Failure of the attack on Syracuse

The naval battle

A NAVAL BATTLE

they threw themselves headlong from their ships and dashed through the water to the land and their camp. "They now suffered what they had done to others at Pylos," wrote Thucydides. "Even now there is a chance," declared the Athenian generals, "even now we have more vessels than the enemy. At break of day we will man them and try to force the passage." But the horrors of the battle had thrown the men into a panic; they refused to go on board the ships.

The Greeks' only hope of safety was to retreat, and perhaps

The Athenians in a panic

make their way to some friendly city; and they began their sorrowful march. The dead lay unburied, the wounded and dying cried to their old friends by name as they passed, and prayed to be taken with them; then called down the anger of the gods upon them as they paid no heed to the appeals. The whole army were in tears; they were in the utmost misery. Demosthenes and part of the army became separated from the rest; but Nicias pushed on. Food gave out, water could not be found. At last they came to a river. They were so wild from thirst that they plunged into it and stood in the shallows, drinking again and again, even though the Syracusans were shooting at them and hurling darts and spears and stones. Men were trampled under foot; they were pierced by the spears of their friends, even by their own spears; they were struck by masses of baggage and swept down stream.

Flaxman

A GREEK SOLDIER LEAVING FOR BATTLE

Heaps of dead bodies lay where the water was shallow, and the river ran red with blood. Then Nicias yielded. "Do what you please with me," he begged, "but spare my men."

Both Nicias and Demosthenes were put to death. The whole Grecian army was captured, save a few who had succeeded in escaping to some friendly city. The prisoners, seven thousand or more, were crowded into the stone quarries. The sun beat down upon them by day; at night they shivered with the cold.

Half a pint of water and a pint of food were given them daily. They died by scores, and the dead bodies lay heaped one upon another. At the end of ten weeks, those who still lived were sold as slaves. Thus ended the expedition that was to have made Athens the ruler of the Mediterranean world. Such is the glory and the splendor of warfare.

SUMMARY

Many leagues were formed among the states.

The Athenians took Melos. They planned an expedition against Sicily under Alcibiades.

To help Egesta was the pretext of the expedition. The Egestæans deceived the Athenians by showing them borrowed treasures.

The ships sailed. At Rhegium the deceit of the Egestæans was discovered The question was whether to collect what the Egestæans had promised, force Selinus to terms, and go home; whether to attack Syracuse at once; or whether to win Sicilian allies and then make an attack.

Alcibiades was recalled to be tried for mutilating the Hermæ, but fled to Sparta and became a traitor to his country.

Sparta came to aid Syracuse.

The Athenians waited, as the soothsayer advised, and their attack failed. They made a disastrous retreat, and the whole army was captured.

SUGGESTIONS FOR WRITTEN WORK

Why did the Athenians wish to overcome Sicily?

A boy describes the sailing of the fleet for Sicily.

What the Syracusans talked about the day before the Corinthian ship arrived.

XVI

THE FALL OF ATHENS

THE traitor Alcibiades had led Athens into the attack upon Sicily, he had shown her enemies how to overcome her powerful fleet **The misery of the Athenians** and her thousands of men, and it was by his advice that they had seized Decelea. The country round about Decelea had been made as bare of food as the sand of the shore. The sheep and cattle had been killed, and more than twenty thousand slaves had deserted. Food could be obtained by the Athenians from the island of Eubœa as usual, but now it could not be brought directly across the strait to Decelea and thence to Athens; it had to come by a long sea voyage around Sunium. This was slow, expensive, and what was

ALCIBIADES
(In the Vatican at Rome)

worse, it was dangerous; for the Spartan ships might dash out at **Their food supply in danger** any moment from behind some sheltering point, and never would the Athenians see either ship or cargo. Their only comfort had lain in the hope that the conquest of Sicily would bring them untold wealth, and that the return of their army would make it possible to drive away the Spartans from Decelea. Then came

the news of the Sicilian defeat. The Athenians had no longer
ships, money, or men, and almost every house was in mourning.
At first they were crushed by the awful disaster; they felt sure
that the Syracusans, the Spartans, the Corinthians, the Bœotians,
every tribe that had ever been envious of their glory, would now
attack them; the colonies would revolt, and they were helpless.
Then they raged at every one who had said a word in favor of
Their courage and determination the expedition; and then, with a magnificent courage and determination, they went to work to make the best of things. They
raised as large an army as possible, and called home every banished man to join it; they sent to Thrace and Macedonia for
timber and built warships; and they cut down the city expenses
to the lowest point. The assembly and the thoughtless multitude
of voters were thoroughly frightened. They were not so sure as
they had been that whatever they wanted to do was wise, and
they appointed ten elderly men to serve as a council.

The Persians had been watching Greece closely, and just at this
time the king, Darius II, issued a declaration claiming that every
foot of land which had been in the hands of his ancestors for even
a moment belonged to him and must pay him tribute. This
would include Attica itself and many of the cities and islands of
the Ægean, indeed, nearly all the Athenian empire. His manner
of making sure of the tribute was simple and easy; he merely sent
an order to the satraps, or governors in Asia Minor to this effect:
"Collect this money for me as best you can." The satraps were
in a great fright. They could not collect the tribute without help,
and they offered to pay well for the aid of Sparta. Now was the
The treaty between Sparta and Persia chance for the firebrand Alcibiades. He helped Chios and other
islands and cities to revolt from Athens, and he arranged a treaty
between the Spartans and the Persians. Against Athens, then,

were the Spartans and their Grecian allies, the Syracusans, the Persians, and many of the cities of the Delian League. Samos remained friendly.

But Alcibiades was becoming rather tired of Sparta, and in spite of all that he had done for them, the Spartans were beginning to be tired of him. When he went to their country, he had Alcibiades goes to Persia shaved off his heavy beard, dressed like a native, had been quiet and grave in manner, lived as simply as any one of them, and even claimed to be fond of black broth. This won the hearts of the Spartans, but after a while he began to do things contrary, not only to the customs, but to the laws, and even committed a crime against the king himself. He expected the Spartans to bear like the Athenians whatever he chose to do; but nevertheless he watched them closely. There came a time when he had reason to believe that his life was in danger. Then he slipped away to the Persian satrap Tissa-pher'nes. Once on Persian soil, he forgot his fondness for black broth; he let his beard grow; he wore the richest and most costly robes that could be obtained; he slept on the softest couches and covered his floors with the thickest carpets; he had his expensive horses, his perfumers, his skillful cooks, and his long train of attendants. The satrap Tissaphernes was not fond of the Greeks, but he was quite dazzled by the flatteries and the brilliant conversation of his new friend. He had beautiful gardens, and the most charming one of all, with fresh green meadows, sparkling streams, and royal pavilions, he named the Garden of Alcibiades.

A PERSIAN NOBLE

But Alcibiades had no idea of becoming a Persian. He dreamed of a return to Athens, and he was planning how to He pleads to return to Athens bring it about. He began by persuading Tissaphernes not to help the Spartans so lavishly. "If you let Sparta crush Athens," he said, "then you will have to fight Sparta. Why not let the two states keep on fighting till they have worn each other out? Then it will be an easy matter to overcome them both." Never was there a shrewder man than the fascinating Alcibiades. He had given the Persians advice that they could not help seeing was wise; he could say to the Athenians that he had done them a good turn with the Persians; and in preventing the Spartans from crushing Athens he had saved himself from ever falling into their victorious hands — and he was terribly afraid of being again in their power. His next move was to send messages to his friends at Samos. "The Persians hate a democracy," he said, "but if Athens were only governed by an oligarchy, I could win their friendship for you, and they would supply you with money. I would gladly return to my own country and cast in my lot with yours." Alcibiades's friends sent men secretly to Athens; and one day the army at Samos were astonished to learn that the government was in the hands of a company of nobles, the Four Hundred, as they were called. Then the soldiers reasoned, "Alcibiades declares that he has had nothing to do with this new government. He can win friends and money for us from the Persians; let us make him general." So it was that, while claiming to be a friend of the Spartans and the Persians, Alcibiades became general of the Athenian army.

The Four Hundred

AN ATHENIAN ARMY GENERAL

A stranger thing than this came to pass a little later. Some Athenian ships were defeated by the Spartans, and Eubœa fell into the hands of Sparta. The Athenians were alarmed and indignant. They threw the blame upon their new government and at once abolished the council of the Four Hundred. Then they began to wonder whom they should make their leader. Alcibiades was already at the head of the army in Samos; he was a successful general, and he had said that he was longing to come home to his own countrymen. In spite of all that he had done, they forgave him and commanded him to return.

Alcibiades invited home

The Spartans had not been blind. They had soon found that Tissaphernes made fine promises, but did not keep them. Another satrap, Phar-na-ba'zus, who ruled in the northern part of Asia Minor, had long been seeking their help to conquer the Greek cities in his province, and especially about the Hellespont. His wishes fell in with those of the Spartans, for if they kept even a small guard at the Hellespont, Athens could no longer get grain from the country about the Black Sea. Now that no food came to her from Eubœa, her only hope was to get it from this region.

The Spartan and Persian forces gathered about the Hellespont. There, too, went the Athenian fleet. They won a victory, a second, a third. Alcibiades was doing his best for the country that he had ruined. Once more gold and silver and arms and prisoners and ships fell into the hands of the Athenians. Once more the Spartans asked for peace; and once more the Athenians, elated by their new successes, refused. Alcibiades continued his victories. Byzantium was in the hands of the enemy; he captured it, and also Chal-ce'don, on the Asiatic side of the Bosphorus. The way to the Black Sea was now clear, and if the ships of the Athenians did not fail them, there need be no lack of grain.

Success of Alcibiades

In spite of the command to return to Athens, the shrewd and cautious Alcibiades had not thought it wise to show himself in his home city; but now in this glory of victory he thought he might venture. His ships were all aglow with flags and shields that he had taken from the enemy; but still he did not land until he saw so many of his friends at the wharf of the Piræus that he felt sure not only of a welcome but also of protection in case of need. It would have been hard for any country not to welcome a general who brought such trophies of victory; but this was the charming, brilliant, eloquent Alcibiades, and the people were wild with delight. They paid no attention to the other generals, but shouted, "Alcibiades! Alcibiades! Alcibiades has come!" They pointed him out to their children. "That is Alcibiades," they said; and then they told of his glorious victories. They crowned him with flowers; they wept for sorrow when they remembered all that they had lost; and they wept for joy when they thought of all that he would gain for them. "If he had been in command, we should not have lost Sicily," they lamented; "but he will make Athens powerful again.' A meeting of the assembly was held, and Alcibiades made a speech. He was grieved, but ready to forgive. They had treated him a little unkindly, he said, but it was his fate and must have been caused by some evil spirit. He talked about their enemies and explained how he expected to get the better of them. The assembly could hardly pass decrees fast enough. They gave him back his estates; they ordered golden crowns for him ; and they put him in command of all their forces.

His triumph-
ant return

Alcibiades received these honors graciously, but as if they were merely his due. He knew how easily the Athenians could be turned, and he meant to have still another hold upon them. His enemies might yet bring up the old charge of mimicking the Eleusinian Mysteries; and he intended to let the ships and the army wait for their commander until he had put himself right with the priests by enabling them to celebrate the Mysteries with all the ancient honors. Since the Spartans had held Decelea, the

His aid to
the priests

journey by land had not been safe, and there had been merely a
hasty voyage to E-leu'sis by sea. Alcibiades sent out a strong
guard, and the procession of priests and others, bearing the image of Dionysus and leading the animals for
sacrifice, marched slowly along the road to Eleusis.
The sacred dances were performed, no detail of the old
rites was neglected, and the celebrants returned
in safety. "Our noble Alcibiades is not only a
great general, but to-day he has filled the place of
a high-priest," said the Athenians; and when he
again sailed from the Piræus, they watched him
out of sight, talking together of the victories
that he would win and the glory he would
surely bring to Athens.

DIONYSUS
(From a painting at Pompeii)

It was but a little while before these devoted Athenians were listening angrily to a
man from the seat of war who reported that
a battle had just been lost, and that it was
all the fault of Alcibiades. The truth was that the commander
had been obliged to leave the army for a short time to get money
to pay his men. He had given strict orders that there should
be no fighting while he was gone; but the officer in charge had
disobeyed and had been beaten in a small engagement. The
Athenians, however, took no pains to learn the exact truth, and
perhaps, even after all their praise of him, they did not really feel
sure of his faithfulness. They called a meeting of the assembly and appointed new generals. Alcibiades feared for his life, Alcibiades
leaves the
left the army, and built himself a castle in Thrace. He could not army
be idle. He picked up men here and there until he had a little
army of his own. Then he made war against the Thracians, who

had no king. If he had had a long life, he might perhaps have been at the head of a state.

The Spartans now sent out an able general, Ly-san'der; and the king of Persia sent out his equally able son Cyrus in the place of Tissaphernes. He had concluded that it was best to help the Spartans generously. Money became plentiful in the Spartan army. Soldiers were paid high wages, and ships were built. The

At the Hellespont

Spartans and Persians were encamped on the Asiatic side of the Hellespont, and the Athenians on the European side, at Æ-gos-pot'a-mi. Every morning the Athenians sailed out and offered battle. The Spartans did not accept the challenge. Then the Athenians returned to their own side of the strait and spent the day wandering about to amuse themselves, and going to Ses'tos, two miles away, for their supplies. Alcibiades was not far distant, and he was watching events at the Hellespont. He rode to the camp and told the Athenian commanders that he did not think it was safe to let the seamen leave their vessels and roam about on the shore; nor was it well to camp where there was no town and no good harbor for their ships, and to keep their supplies so far away. He advised them to remove to Sestos. No officer need have felt ashamed to receive advice from so successful a commander, but the generals replied curtly, "We are giving orders now, not you. Begone!"

Alcibiades went away, the Spartans still refused to fight, and the Athenians became more and more careless. Suddenly the

The battle of Ægospota-mi, 405 B.C.

Spartan and Persian ships swept across the strait. Only one general was on the watch. He gave the signal to man the vessels, but the sailors had gone to Sestos, and only nine of the one hundred and eighty ships could be fully manned. There was hardly an attempt to resist. The Spartans had little to do but to tow the captured vessels across the strait. Eight or ten ships escaped; the rest of the fleet and thousands of men were captured. All among them who were Athenians, about four thousand, were at once put to death.

When the awful news came to Athens, every one realized that the empire had vanished and that Athens itself must fall. The ships of Lysander blocked the Piræus. The troops of the Spartans and their allies surrounded the city. A few weeks passed, then came famine and unconditional surrender. The fall of Athens, 404 B.C.

What should be the fate of the Athenians? The allies discussed the question. "Tear down the city to its foundations and sell every man, woman, and child as a slave,"demanded the angry Thebans and Bœotians. "We will never consent to put out one of the eyes of Greece," replied the Spartans. This sounded merciful, but there

RUINS OF ATHENS

were some who whispered that the Spartans were shrewd rather than generous; for if Athens was utterly destroyed, either Thebes or Corinth would probably become stronger than Sparta herself. At length they decided that the Long Walls and the fortifications Fate of the Athenians of the Piræus should be leveled, that only twelve ships should be left to the conquered city, and that she should agree to obey the orders of Sparta on land and sea.

In Athens there was heart-breaking sorrow. Loved ones were gone from every home. There were poverty and starvation and utter misery. At the Piræus women were playing the flute, there were singing and dancing and all sorts of merry-making; for men were tearing down the mighty walls. "Greece is free! Liberty has come to the Greeks!" they shouted gleefully. High up on the Acropolis rose the Parthenon, strong and beautiful. Near it stood the statue of Athene, serene and stately. Around it was a land in ruins, an empire overthrown.

SUMMARY

The Athenians were almost crushed by the Sicilian disaster.

Darius II claimed nearly all the Athenian empire. Alcibiades arranged a treaty between Persia and Sparta.

Alcibiades fled to Tissaphernes, but planned to return to Athens.

The Athenian government fell into the hands of the Four Hundred. The Athenian soldiers made Alcibiades general.

Spartans, Persians, and Athenians gathered at the Hellespont. Alcibiades won several victories. He was welcomed in Greece. He enabled the priests to celebrate the Mysteries. He was blamed for a lost battle and left the army.

The Spartan Lysander and the Persian Cyrus overcame the Athenians at Ægospotami. Athens surrendered. Her fortifications were leveled.

SUGGESTIONS FOR WRITTEN WORK

Two Athenians discuss the Sicilian disaster.

Alcibiades describes his life among the Spartans.

An Athenian describes the return of Alcibiades.

XVII

WHEN SPARTA RULED

SPARTA was now in command, and all the cities that were in her power watched anxiously to see what she would do. For twenty-seven years, from the beginning of the war to its close, she had been saying to them "Athens is a tyrant, and Sparta is striving to set you free" Now they learned that Sparta's idea of freedom was for her to do what she chose and force the other states to yield to her. The first thing that she did in each city was to give it a Spartan governor, with ten men friendly to his plans as magistrates, and enough Spartan soldiers to compel the citizens to be obedient. The

How Sparta made cities free

MARKET-PLACE OF SPARTA

(In the background is the citadel; in the foreground, the statue of Hermes with the infant Dionysus; in the rear of the open court is the statue of the Spartan people; on the right is the Persian hall, adorned with the spoils of the Persian War)

Ægean cities were especially helpless. They had thought it hard to be obliged to pay tribute to Athens, but now they had to

Helplessness of the Ægean cities

pay not only the tribute, but also for the support of the governor and his soldiers.

Sparta suddenly forgot that Athens was "one of the two eyes of Greece," and treated her far more severely than any other city. Ten magistrates were not enough for the Athenians, — they must have thirty, besides the Spartan governor and a large body of Spartan soldiers. The Thirty Tyrants, as they came to be called, chose three thousand men who they were sure would stand by them, and took away all arms from the rest of the citizens. Then they had no fear of gods or men. They put to death all who had worked against them during the war, all those against whom they had any grudge, and enough of the wealthier men to supply themselves liberally with money. The wretched Athenians said to one another even then, "Alcibiades will not bear this; he will surely find some way to help us"; but it was not long before they heard that Alcibiades had been assassinated. Then, indeed, they were hopeless, and hundreds fled from the city. The other states were angry at the selfishness of Sparta, and were ready to give the fugitives a home. Even the Thebans, who had been such bitter enemies of the Athenians, welcomed them. Just as soon as the little company of exiles had grown large enough to make the venture, they crossed the border of Attica and made a stand against

the Thirty. Xen'o-phon, a disciple of Socrates, wrote, "The Thirty, quite dejected and solitary, sat together in council." They might well be "quite dejected," for this was the beginning of the overthrow of their rule.

No nation is quite the same at the end of a long war as at the beginning. During the Peloponnesian War the members of each party in Athens had been so sure that they were in the right that they hated the other political parties most bitterly, and had come to feel that whatever act brought them their own way was the proper course to follow. The philosopher Socrates had fought fearlessly for Athens, and he loved his city; but he saw that it was more important to do right than for any party to get what it wanted; and that to be honest and good was better than to pay sacrifices to the gods. Such teachings as these did not please the people, who meant to have their own way no matter what happened. At length he was brought into court and accused of not worshiping the gods and of giving false teaching to young men. He

SOCRATES
(From a bust in the Vatican Gallery at Rome)

was condemned to die, or, as he said, "to depart to some happy state of the blessed." Several of his followers were with him

Last days of Socrates

DEATH OF SOCRATES

during the last days of his life, and one of them, named Plato, wrote an account of the teacher's words and acts. When the cup of poison was brought him, he drank it as quietly as if it had been wine. His

His fearless
death

disciples burst into tears. Plato says, "I did not weep for him, but for my own fortune in being deprived of such a friend." At the last, when all supposed that the poison had taken effect, Socrates called to one of the young men, "Cri'to, we owe a cock to Æs-cu-la'-pi-us; pay it, therefore, and do not neglect it." Æsculapius was the god to whom a man who was grateful for his recovery from illness made a sacrifice; and Socrates was so sure of a nobler, happier life to come that he felt as if giving up his life on earth was only passing from sickness to health.

ÆSCULAPIUS
(In the Vatican Gallery at Rome)

The following is a bit of the wisdom of Socrates. One An'ti-pho wished to draw away the followers of the philosopher. Therefore he came to Socrates one day when they were present, and said, "I thought that those who studied philosophy were to become happier than other men; but you seem to have reaped from philosophy fruits of an opposite kind; at least you live in a way in which no slave would continue to live with his master: you eat food, and drink drink, of the worst kind; you wear a dress, not only bad, but the same both summer and winter, and you continue shoeless and coatless. Money, which cheers men when they receive it, and enables those who possess it to live more generously and pleasantly, you do not take; and if, therefore, as teachers in other professions make their pupils imitate themselves, you also shall produce a similar effect on your fol-

He is called
a teacher of
wretched-
ness

lowers, you must consider yourself but a teacher of wretched-
ness." Socrates replied quietly, "You, Antipho, resemble one His idea of
who thinks that happiness consists in luxury and extravagance; happiness
but I think that to want nothing is to resemble the gods, and
that to want as little as possible is to make the nearest approach
to the gods; that the divine nature is perfection, and that to be
nearest to the divine nature is to be nearest to perfection."

The enemies of Socrates did not forget to remind the judges
that Alcibiades and Crit'i-as, the chief of the Thirty Tyrants, Plato, fifth
had been among his pupils; but there was more than one of his and fourth
devoted followers who became an honor to Socrates and to his B. C.
country. Plato lived
half a century after
the death of his be-
loved teacher, and
became even more
famous as a philoso-
pher. He wrote on
the deepest subjects,
but with so much hu-
mor and fancy and
sweetness, that peo-
ple began to claim
that he was a de-

THE SO-CALLED PRISON OF SOCRATES AT ATHENS
(From a photograph)

scendant of Apollo, the god of eloquence. Disciples flocked
around him as around Socrates, and he used to talk with them His fame
and lecture in his garden close by the Ac-a-de'me. The story has popularity
come down to us that some strangers who met him at the Olympian games were so pleased with him that they accepted gladly
his invitation to visit him in Athens. When it was nearly time

for their visit to come to an end, they said, "But will you not introduce us to your famous namesake, the philosopher Plato?" They were surprised indeed when their host replied simply, "I am the person whom you wish to see."

Another follower of Socrates was Xenophon, who was a philosopher, a military commander, and a historian. When Socrates

Xenophon, fifth and fourth centuries B. C.

Raphael

SCHOOL OF ATHENS

(Plato with Aristotle beside him is lecturing; Diogenes lies on the steps; Alcibiades and Xenophon are listening to Socrates on the left of the platform)

was in prison, Xenophon was just returning from a remarkable expedition that was planned by Cyrus of Persia. After the Peloponnesian War was over, Cyrus sent envoys to Sparta to ask the Spartans that they behave toward him as he had behaved toward them. By this he meant that he wanted to borrow some Grecian soldiers. His brother, Ar-tax-erx'es II, was on the throne

Cyrus asks help of Sparta

of Persia, but many thought it belonged to Cyrus, and he had
raised an army of 100,000 men to help him get possession of it.
He knew how well the Greeks fought, and it is no wonder
that he was eager to hire them. There were thousands of men in **He hires Greek soldiers**
Greece who knew little of any other life than that of the soldier,
and they were ready to fight for any one who would pay their
wages. They would not, however, have agreed to go to the heart

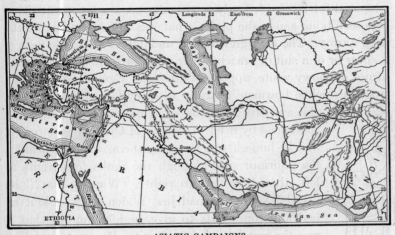

ASIATIC CAMPAIGNS
(Dotted line shows route of Ten Thousand ; unbroken line, Alexander's marches)

of Asia; so they were tricked into making the march by being **His deception**
told that Cyrus wanted them to help subdue some rebels in
Pi-sid'i-a, on the southern coast of Asia Minor. They crossed
the Ægean Sea, landed near Samos, and set out cheerfully toward
Pisidia. But Pisidia seemed to be a long way off, and at length
they began to suspect some trickery. By and by Cyrus and his
troops met them, and he finally admitted that they were on
their way to Bab-y-lo'ni-a and were to fight, not a few rebels,

but the king of the mighty Persian empire. They were already well into Persia, and it was almost as dangerous to try to retreat as to go forward. Cyrus promised them generous wages and they agreed to go on.

One day, just before noon, a man came galloping up to the army at full speed, crying out, first in Persian and then in Greek, "The king is coming, the king is coming, with a vast army all prepared for battle!" Early in the afternoon a low white cloud was seen lying across the plain. That was the dust made by the

The army of Artaxerxes arrives

king's army. The dust grew darker and darker; then the flash of a spear or of a suit of brazen armor could be seen. Cavalry, with armor of snowy white, appeared; troops of Egyptians with long wooden shields; bowmen; chariots with scythes projecting from

PERSIAN WARRIOR

the axle-tree; nations upon nations, each one in a solid mass by itself. The lines of Cyrus were forming, and he himself was watching them, when he heard a low murmur pass through the ranks from right to left, then from left to right. "What is that?" he asked. Xenophon had just ridden up to ask if he had any commands to give, and he replied that it was the watchword, "Jupiter the Preserver, and Victory." "I accept it as a good omen," said Cyrus, "and may it be so."

Cyrus slain

The omen proved false. It is true that the valiant Greeks won the battle, but Cyrus was slain. "Give up your arms," the king commanded. "Victors do not give up their arms," replied the Greeks. The king did not care to fight again. He wanted rather to get rid of those troublesome foreigners, and he thought it would be a good plan to let them wander off into the country and starve. Their generals were slain through a trick;

and the Greeks were left in an enemy's country, at least one thousand miles from home. They had no guides, no commander, and little knowledge of the land save that there were many rivers and mountains. They were in despair. Night came and they lay on the ground, longing for their families and their own country. Xenophon had gone to Persia with the army, not as a soldier, and with no idea of fighting the king, but only to win advancement with Cyrus. As he lay on the ground, he made up his mind that since no one else took the lead, it was left for him to do something. He hesitated because there were so many older men than he; then he said to himself, "Surely, I shall never be any older if I give myself up to the enemy to-day." This was soon after midnight. In the darkness he called together the captains and they planned as best they could. "Do you tell the army," they said; and in the first gray of the morning Xenophon put on his best armor and his finest accoutrements and stood before the ten thousand men. He told them how brave their forefathers had been, and that they could surely make their way home. They must burn their baggage, saving only what was needed of meat and drink and arms. "If we are victorious, we ought to look upon the enemy as our baggage-carriers," he said.

Xenophon arouses the officers

The soldiers forgot their discouragement. They burned all the baggage they could spare, chose new generals, — of course Xenophon was one, — ate their breakfast with good cheer, and started on one of the most remarkable of retreats. They plodded over burning plains, waded through swiftly flowing rivers, climbed rugged hills, pushed on through mountain-passes where snowdrifts were a fathom deep and the keenest of winter winds whistled around them. Sometimes they had food and sometimes no food. Sometimes they were allowed to pass through a district

The retreat of the Ten Thousand

in peace, sometimes they were attacked on all sides. If they could only come to the sea! they thought, for then the way to friends and home would be easy. At length Xenophon heard one day

XENOPHON

a great shout from the men in advance. It grew louder and louder. It did not sound like a battle-cry, and yet there might be a foe in front of them, — no one could tell. He sprang upon his horse and galloped up the hill. Behold, on the horizon, far away to the north, lay a line of shining water, the Euxine Sea. "The Sea, the Sea!" shouted the soldiers. Those sturdy warriors burst into tears, they threw their arms around one another's necks, they embraced their generals and captains. The native who had led them up the hill stood by. They gave him a horse, a silver cup, a Persian robe, and ten gold coins. They raised a mound, as had been done at Marathon, and on it they laid ox-hides and staves, and shields taken from the enemy. In three days the Ten Thousand were at the Greek city of Treb'i-zond. The citizens welcomed them and gave them oxen and wine and barley meal, and celebrated games in honor of the kindness of the gods. Xenophon himself wrote the account of this retreat of the Ten Thousand who fought their way for a thousand miles through the enemy's country to the sea.

The return of the Ten Thousand

Xenophon, too, as well as Plato, loved Socrates, and wrote what he could remember of his master's teachings. After giving him the warmest praise, he closed with the words, "If any one disapproves of my opinion, let him compare the conduct of others with that of Socrates, and determine accordingly."

The march of the Ten Thousand showed the Greeks that the enormous Persian empire was really a big unwieldy realm, without life or energy; and Sparta was somewhat pleased when the Greek coast cities begged for help against Tissaphernes, who was making ready to punish every city that had been friendly to Cyrus. After a little fighting between the Spartans and Tissaphernes, the Spartan king A-ges-i-la'us formed the plan of sweeping through Persia and conquering the overgrown dominion. He was so successful that it really began to seem as if he might be able to carry out his plan; but the crafty Persians could scheme if they could not fight. They knew that the other Greeks hated Sparta for her tyranny and selfishness, and now they offered ships and men, and contrived to induce Corinth, Athens, Thebes, and Argos to unite against her. This was the beginning of the Corinthian War, which lasted for eight years. Much of the fighting was done in Corinth, but at last there was a great naval battle off Cni'dus, in Asia Minor. Then there came a sorry day for Sparta, for the whole Spartan fleet was destroyed. A little later there was more joy in Athens than there had been for many a day, for by the aid of Persian money the first stones were put in place for the rebuilding of the Long Walls and the fortifications of the Piræus.

Sparta plans the conquest of Persia

The Corinthian War, 395–387 B.C

Battle of Cnidus, 394 B.C.

CNIDUS AND ITS TWO HARBORS
(Many ancient triremes anchored in these harbors)

The Athenians were happy, but their allies were jealous. "Why should we fight if Athens is to have the reward?" they questioned. Sparta, too, began to be uncomfortable. "Why should we try to protect the Greek colonies if all that our work amounts to is to help Athens?" they grumbled. There was nothing to do but to make peace, and with their usual selfishness they made a treaty, **The Peace of Antalcidas, 387 B.C.** called the Peace of An-tal'ci-das from the name of the ambassador, which gave the Greek cities of Asia to the Persians. Almost worse than this was a sentence in the treaty which declared that the Persian king and the Spartans would fight any state that refused to obey its terms. This really meant that Sparta was ready to unite with Persia against any part of her own country.

Sparta not only made a shameful treaty, but she behaved even more shamefully in carrying it out. She still claimed that she was giving freedom to the Greeks, and she not only set to work to force every city that was ruling another to give up that control, but she broke up any friendly union of towns that she fancied **Sparta destroys Mantinea** might some day be of injury to her. She thought that the people of Mantinea in Arcadia did not approve of her course, and she tore down their walls and forced the citizens to separate and settle five little villages. The government of Greece was really a sort of tyranny, and Sparta was the tyrant. A Spartan general was marching through the friendly city of Thebes when **A Theban betrays his city to Sparta** a Theban said to him privately, "The other party hates the Spartans, but ours is friendly to you. I will conduct you into the citadel; Thebes will then be in your power, and you will not forget us." It was a hot summer noon, and there were few people in the streets to oppose, and soon the Spartan general was in control of Thebes. When news of this reached the Spartans, they were indignant, not because he had done so wicked a deed, but because he had done it without orders from the state. Then said

King Agesilaus, "The point is whether he has done harm or good to Sparta. If harm, he ought to be punished; but if good, it is an old rule that a man may do such a thing of his own accord." They concluded that it was good for Sparta, and therefore they kept the citadel.

Many Thebans of the opposite party fled from the city in fear for their lives. Among them was one Pe-lop'i-das. He used to say to the other exiles, "It is dishonorable to be contented with saving our own lives; we ought to be striving to free our city." At length he aroused them, and a plan was made to deliver Thebes. Pelopidas and some others of the younger men dressed as peasants and stole into the city by different ways. It was so cold and snowy that most people were in their houses, but some friends of the exiles were on the watch to lead them to the place of meeting. When evening had come, they put on the dresses of women over their armor, with heavy wreaths of pine and poplar falling over their foreheads to hide their bearded faces. So disguised, they went to the place where the leaders of the party that had betrayed their city were banqueting, and slew the chief ones among them. Pelopidas threw open the jails to free those who were true to Thebes. Now the lights began to shine out from the windows of the houses; the streets were full of people; there was confusion and shouting everywhere, for no one knew just what had happened. When morning had come, the loyal Thebans called the people together. Then Pelopidas and the other exiles, his friend E-pam-i-non'das, and the priests of the temples stood before the assembly. "Arouse yourselves," cried the priests, "for the gods and your country!" The whole assembly sprang to their feet like one man, and shouted with joy. They marched straight to the citadel. The Spartans who held it were of differ-

Pelopidas plans to free Thebes

The Spartans surrender the citadel

ent stamp from those of Thermopylæ, and they surrendered at once. One place after another followed the example of Thebes. The Spartans punished the governors who surrendered, but the surrenders did not cease.

Athens founds a new league

Then Athens began to dream of a return of her own greatness. She founded a new association of states that was far better than the Delian League, for the states were to hold equal rank and the money collected was to be used for the benefit of all. This was so fair an association that it might have endured but for the same old trouble, one state's jealousy of another. Now it was the Athenians that were becoming so jealous of Thebes that they decided to make peace with Sparta.

Sparta still declared that she was freeing the Bœotian cities, but one day the Spartan army were surprised to see a Theban

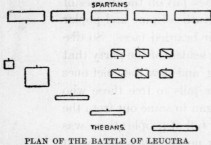

PLAN OF THE BATTLE OF LEUCTRA
(The Spartan king was on the right of the Spartan line)

army march out to meet them. The Spartans arranged their men in the same old way that they had followed for generations, and advanced toward the enemy in a long line, twelve men deep. Epaminondas, who led the Thebans, reasoned, "The best warriors will be around the king, and if we can defeat them, the rest will be an easy matter." Therefore he did not make his line of the same depth, but arranged the ranks opposite the king fifty men deep. No line twelve deep could be expected to withstand the attack of a line fifty deep, and although Sparta had more men, she met the worst defeat in all her history, for her army was beaten in a fair fight by a much smaller force. This was the battle of Leuc'tra.

The battle of Leuctra, 371 B.C.

When the news was brought to Sparta that their men had been beaten by a smaller number, the ephors knew well that the Greeks would never fear them again; they had lost the leadership of their country. If the Spartans had been Athenians, they would have wept and moaned, but being Spartans, they bore their loss in the old Spartan fashion. "Let the games go on," bade the ephors, for they were in the midst of a festival. All the usual ceremonies were observed, and the ephors themselves stayed until the last contest and the last dance were ended. It was the Spartan custom to shame in every way possible any soldier who had fled from a battle. He was obliged to shave one half his beard and leave the other half uncut. He must wear shabby clothes covered with patches of different colors. He was never allowed to hold office, and any Spartan girl who married such a man was looked upon as having disgraced herself. So many had fled from the battle of Leuctra that the Spartans did not dare to treat them in this fashion; but the relatives of those who had died went about the streets with an air of pride, and entered the temples to give thanks for the courage of their friends. The relatives of those who had escaped from the battle wore sorrowful faces, and walked through the city with their heads bowed, or even shut themselves up altogether, as was the Spartan custom in time of deepest mourning. So it was that Sparta bore the defeat that destroyed her dream of becoming the ruler of Greece.

How Sparta bore defeat

Pride and shame of relatives

GREEK WOMEN
(From a group in the Louvre)

SUMMARY

Sparta enslaved the cities that she had claimed to be setting free; but the " Thirty " in Athens were overthrown.

Socrates made enemies and was condemned to die. Plato and Xenophon were his pupils.

Cyrus hired Greek soldiers on a false pretense and led them into Asia. They overcame Artaxerxes II in battle; but he slew the generals and left them to wander away and starve. Xenophon urged them to make a brave retreat. They did so, and at length they came to the sea. Then their way to Greece was easy.

This "March of the Ten Thousand" showed the weakness of Persia, and Sparta planned the conquest of the country. The Persians induced Corinth, Athens, Thebes, and Argos to unite against Sparta. This was the beginning of the Corinthian War. The Spartan fleet was destroyed at the battle of Cnidus. Persian money helped to rebuild the Athenian walls. The Peace of Antalcidas was made, by which Sparta agreed to unite with Persia to punish any state that broke the treaty.

Sparta became tyrant of Greece. She seized the citadel of Thebes. Many of the Thebans fled. At length Pelopidas and others returned and drove out the Spartans. Other places also yielded.

Athens formed an association of states and finally made peace with Sparta.

The Thebans under Epaminondas won at Leuctra, and the Spartans were no longer the leaders of Greece.

SUGGESTIONS FOR WRITTEN WORK

One of Plato's guests tells the story of his visit to Athens.

A soldier of Xenophon describes the last day of the march.

How Pelopidas took Thebes.

XVIII

WHEN THEBES WAS IN POWER

THE cities that Sparta had treated so tyrannically were as quick as she to see that her power had vanished. The Mantineans left their little settlements in the country, went straight back to the site of their city, and began to rebuild the walls. A little earlier Sparta would have dispatched an army at once to punish such audacity, but now all that she dared to do was to send to the Mantineans a man whom they had always liked and beg them to wait a while. "Only wait," he pleaded; "the Spartans will soon give formal consent. If you will wait, they will even pay for rebuilding the walls." "It is impossible," returned the magistrates, "for a resolution has been passed to rebuild them at once." "Will you not at least permit me to speak to the general assembly?" asked the envoy; but the magistrate said "No," and the building of the walls went on.

Mantinea had paid no attention to the wishes of Sparta, but that was a small matter compared with what the fallen state had still to endure. Sparta had been so selfish and tyrannical that many states were eager to make sure that she could no longer oppress them. After the victory at Leuctra, Thebes was looked upon as the most powerful city, and Epaminondas was without question the greatest military commander in the land. Under him as general a large army invaded the Peloponnesus to help two states, Arcadia and Messenia. Whatever Epaminondas undertook, he did thoroughly. He was not satisfied with marching

Epaminon-
das unites
Arcadia and
founds
Megalopolis

through Arcadia, but he actually founded a city. He chose a broad fertile plain for its site and induced the Arcadians to unite their village communities into the new city of Meg-a-lop'o-lis, that is, the great city. Now that the Arcadians had a capital and could take refuge within her walls, it would not be an easy matter for Sparta to oppress her, even if no Theban army was on guard. Thus Arcadia was made independent; but Epaminondas did even more than this for Messenia. This country was the

STATUE OF VICTORY, RESTORED
(Made for the Messenians by the sculptor
Pæonius)

old home of the Helots before they were enslaved by the Spartans. Those whom the Athenians had invited to settle at Naupactus had been driven from this refuge by the Spartans at the close of the Peloponnesian War. They had fled to Italy, Sicily, Africa, wherever they could find homes. When they heard that Epaminondas had marched into Messenia and that now their mother country was free, there was a glad home-coming. By land and by sea, in large bands, in little companies, in families, even one by one, they poured into Messenia;

The Mes-
senians re-
turn home

for once more they had a country and a home. The land reëchoed with songs of rejoicing and shouts of happiness. There were sacrifices of thanksgiving to the gods; and there was also much hard work, since for the Messenians, too, Epaminondas had founded a city, Mes-se'ne. It was to stand on the side of Mount

Ithome, and its walls were yet to be built. No town without walls could hope to resist an attack of the Spartans; and the Messenians began their building as gladly as Athens had begun to rebuild the fortifications of the Piræus. A traveler who saw these walls five hundred years later declared that they were the strongest he had ever found. They were "built of solid stone," he said, "and well supplied with towers and buttresses."

Epaminondas aided by Pelopidas had made Thebes the ruling state of Greece. One would have expected that when he returned with his victorious army, he would at least receive a cordial welcome. Instead of that, he was met with a charge of disobedience to the laws of the country. The successes in the Peloponnesus had been won, it seemed, during the last four months, and the enemies of the generals asserted that they had kept the army away from Thebes four months beyond the time for which the command had been given to them. The penalty for such an offense was death. Epaminondas met the charge patiently, and after his acquittal did not even try to punish his enemies. *The base in gratitude to Epaminondas*

Pelopidas had declared that "wherever Epaminondas was, there was no need of any other general"; but there was need of a skillful commander in Thessaly, and thither Pelopidas was sent. The trouble was that the tyrant of one Thessalian city was forcing the other cities to obey him. The ruler of Macedonia, too, was trying to gain power in Thessaly. Pelopidas was as successful in the north as Epaminondas had been in the south, and before long he went home to report that the cities were free from the tyrant and that he had received hostages from the ruler of Macedonia. *Pelopidas in Thessaly and Macedonia*

Thus far Thebes had been making cities free, and they were glad to receive her aid. No one doubted that she was the most

powerful state in Greece; but when she sent Pelopidas to the
Persian king to claim that she instead of Sparta was the chief
of the Greek cities, they were angry, and some of Sparta's old
allies were willing to help her against Thebes. The result was
that Epaminondas had to make other expeditions into the

Epaminondas attacks Sparta

Peloponnesus. On the last he planned to attack Sparta herself.
He "would have taken the city like a bird's nest deserted," said
Xenophon, if King Agesilaus, who had marched out to meet the
invaders, had not hurried home by a shorter route to oppose the
"fire-breathing Thebans." Epaminondas knew that the Spartans would defend their city like wolves at bay, and he wisely
retreated into Arcadia. The
Spartans pursued, and a battle was fought in the valley
of Mantinea. Here Epaminondas played the old game of the
Spartans at Ægospotami, and
deceived them as completely
as they had deceived the Athenians. He ordered his men to
pile their arms and apparently
begin to encamp. Then, when
his foes were entirely off their
guard, he suddenly drew up
his lines and advanced upon
them. The Spartans and their

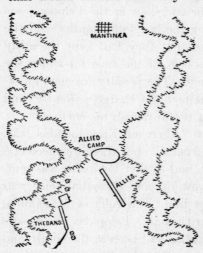

BATTLEFIELD OF MANTINEA

Battle of Mantinea, 362 B. C.

allies were as dazed as the Athenians had been in the naval
battle. They ran about wildly, one fastening on a breastplate,
another bridling his horse, and all of them acting, not like the
Spartans of old who were wont to advance to battle steadily and

cheerfully, but, as Xenophon declared, "more like men going to suffer some harm than to inflict any on others." This time it was not the Spartans but the Thebans who advanced "steadily and cheerfully." Epaminondas had arranged part of his cavalry in a phalanx, and they cut through the Spartan ranks "like a ship of war with its beak directed against the enemy," said Xenophon, perhaps with that very naval battle of Ægospotami in mind as he wrote. Epaminondas won the victory, but he himself was slain. His last thoughts were for his country. Pelopidas had been killed in battle two years before, and now, when Epaminondas asked for one and another who might perhaps have taken his place, the reply was ever, "He has been slain. "Then you must make peace with the enemy," he said, and closed his eyes in death.

Epaminondas slain

The glory of Thebes was a one-man power. It was Epaminondas who had made her great. He had been her general, her leader, her counselor. Now he was gone, and in one day she fell from her proud position as the leading state of Greece.

The fall of Thebes

SUMMARY

The Mantineans scorned Sparta and rebuilt their walls.

Epaminondas united Arcadia, and founded the city of Megalopolis; he freed the Messenians and founded Messene. Aided by Pelopidas, he made Thebes the ruling state of Greece.

Pelopidas freed the cities in Thessaly.

Thebes demanded that Persia regard her as the chief state of Greece. The Greeks were angry, and several states united against her.

Epaminondas overcame Sparta at Mantinea, but was slain. Thebes was no longer the leading state of Greece.

SUGGESTIONS FOR WRITTEN WORK

A Spartan reports what the Mantineans said when they were asked to delay building their wall.

A Messenian tells what Epaminondas had done for him and his countrymen.

A soldier describes the battle of Mantinea.

XIX

PHILIP OF MACEDONIA

So it was that, first Argos, then Athens, Sparta, Thebes, became in turn the leading state of Greece. Their selfishness and jealousy of one another had wasted their wealth and the lives of their citizens, and they were exhausted. There could not have been a better time for a bold, shrewd man, who knew how to work with caution and skill, to become master of the whole country.

Greece exhausted by wars

Such a man was on the throne of Macedonia, the country lying to the north and northeast of Greece. The Macedonians had no artists, no talented writers, no brilliant orators, no schools of philosophy. The Greeks of the south admitted that they were of Greek blood, but laughed at their rude, unpolished manners and their homely fashion of speaking. The man who sat on the throne, Philip II, was keenly alive to all these differences. He had been a boy of fifteen when Pelopidas came to Macedonia and carried him to Thebes as a hostage. There he had stayed for three years, possibly in the house of Epaminondas's father. However that may be, he certainly had an opportunity to learn how the Greeks lived, how they carried on war, and how war might sometimes be avoided by diplomacy. He learned to speak

Philip in Thebes

and write Greek like a Theban; his language became not only correct but eloquent. He knew it was possible that he might some day rule Macedonia, and he evidently kept his eyes and ears open to learn everything that might be of value to him and help him carry out an astonishing scheme that probably was in his mind even then. His ambition

When the time came for him to wear the crown of his father, he began by forming a standing army, and he very wisely invited his most troublesome subjects to join it, — the half-civilized tribes that lived far up in the hills. Thus far Macedonia had made no attempt to be powerful. It had been hardly more than a piece of land through which armies might march between Greece and Asia. If war arose, it had made friends with the side that seemed inclined to be most troublesome. The first part of Philip's scheme was to

MACEDONIAN CAVALRYMAN

make Macedonia so strong that other countries would be eager to make friends with her. Therefore he trained and drilled his soldiers until they formed the best army in the world. He had learned in Thebes how the famous Theban phalanx was formed, but he was not satisfied with even what was looked upon as a wonderful invention; he planned a somewhat different arrangement for the foot-soldiers. In this the men were placed sixteen deep, with three feet between the ranks. The spears were twenty-one feet long, and each man held his weapon fifteen feet from the point. The spears of the fifth rank, then, projected three feet in front of the first rank of men; those of the fourth rank pro- The Macedonian phalanx jected six feet, and so on. It was not easy to keep the phalanx in shape on rough, uneven ground, but on a level no troops could withstand its attack.

When Philip's army was ready, he began his conquests; not by going into Greece, however, — he was too wise for that. He

aimed first at Thrace and Chalcidice. On the border between Thrace and Macedonia was the city of Amphipolis, and he meant to take it. Athens and O-lyn'thus would have united to defend it, but

THE MACEDONIAN PHALANX

Philip takes Amphipolis, 357 B.C.

Philip had no idea of doing more fighting than was necessary; so he promised to give Amphipolis to Athens. By that means he took the city without any interference. He kept Amphipolis instead of giving it to Athens, but gave another city to Olynthus. That broke up any union that might have been formed between Athens and Olynthus. A very crafty man was

A MACEDONIAN SOLDIER WITH THE LONG SPEAR

He seizes Thracian gold mines

Philip II of Macedonia. Of course he did not stop with Amphipolis. A little way over the Thracian line were some rich gold mines. What was to hinder him from taking them? He marched on with his invincible army, and soon he had all the money that he wanted. He could hire soldiers to assault a city, or — for there were at least two parties in every one — he could bribe one party to give up the city to him. There is a story that he once inquired whether a certain fortress could be taken. "It is inaccessible," was the reply. "Is it so inaccessible that not even an ass laden with gold can mount to it?" he questioned.

Philip took other places in the north, and no one opposed him. Athens was the strongest of the Grecian states, and Athens had all she could manage with the cities of the new league, formed after Thebes had been freed from Sparta. They objected as much as those of the old Delian League to being treated by Athens as if they were her subjects; and Athens, in spite of all that she had been through, had not learned that it would be wiser to treat them in any other way. They had revolted, and what is known as the Social War had followed.

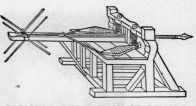

CATAPULT, THE CANNON OF PHILIP'S TIME

(This large bow would shoot iron-pointed arrows weighing from ten to three hundred pounds nearly half a mile)

Still, even when the Social War had come to an end, the Athenians seemed blind to what was going on in the north. One man in the city, however, had his eyes open; but in spite of all his eloquence he could not make the Athenians see the danger that was at hand. This man was Demosthenes, one of the world's greatest orators.

Demosthenes as a child was the last boy one would have selected to make into an orator. He stammered, he had a weak voice, he lost his breath, he could not pronounce the letter r. Then, too, he was awkward, he hunched up his left shoulder continually, and when he became excited or interested, he twisted his face into all sorts of queer shapes. Nevertheless, he was determined to become as great an orator as was a speaker to whom he had once listened, and to be applauded as heartily

His first
speech a
failure

as was that man. When he was older, he seized the first opportunity of speaking in public to the people. They were not persuaded, but they were certainly entertained; and they stood laughing at the young man who threw himself about so violently, confused his arguments, and gasped so for breath that they could not always understand what he was trying to say.

Demosthenes was so dejected that he went out of the city and

wandered down to the Piræus, wondering if he ever should succeed. He tried again, but he made quite as bad a failure. "Why is it," he asked an actor friend, "that though I work so hard on my orations, the people would rather listen to a drunken sailor or any ignorant fellow than me?" The only answer made by his friend was "Won't you repeat to me some passage from Euripides or Sophocles?" Demosthenes obeyed; then the actor repeated the same passage, but with such dignity, such appropriate gestures, and such evident appreciation of every thought, that it became a different thing. Then Demosthenes understood what his friend meant

DEMOSTHENES
(From a statue in the Vatican
Gallery at Rome)

The lesson
of the actor

namely, that no matter how much one has studied a subject or how well his speech has been composed, it will never convince an audience unless it is also well spoken.

There did not seem much hope that Demosthenes would ever succeed, but he was made of too good stuff to give up. He built an underground study to which he would go to exercise his voice and practice gestures. For fear he should be tempted to go out, he would sometimes shave one half of his head so that he could not appear in public. To break up his stammering, he spoke with pebbles in his mouth. To strengthen his voice to overpower the noise of the assemblies of people, he declaimed on the seashore, trying his best to overmatch the tumult of the ocean. He learned to control his breath by delivering speeches while scrambling up steep and rugged hills. He hung a naked sword so that the least movement of the unruly left shoulder would result in a prick. He practiced before a mirror in order to learn not to twist and distort his face. He even overcame the annoying letter *r*. With all this he did not forget to pay more pains than ever to the composition of his orations. He even copied over and over the speeches in Thucydides's history, trying to learn to do as well. And he became such a speaker that for two thousand years he has stood among the greatest orators of the world.

His struggle to become an orator

Such was the man who told the Athenians that Philip of Macedonia was planning to conquer Greece. His speeches against Philip were called Phi-lip'pics. They were so fierce and so bitter that even now an especially savage and relentless speech against a person is often called a philippic. In these orations Demosthenes did his best to arouse his countrymen. "What season, indeed," he demanded, "what opportunity do you wait for more favorable than the present, or when will you exert your vigor if not now, my countrymen? Has not this man seized all those places that were ours? Should he become master of this country, too, must we not sink into the lowest state of infamy? Are not

The Philippics of Demosthenes

they whom we have promised to assist whenever they are engaged in war, now attacked themselves? Is he not our enemy? Is he not in possession of our dominions? Is he not a barbarian? Is he not every base thing words can express? If we are insensible to all this, if we almost aid his designs — heavens! can we then ask to whom the consequences are owing?"

But the days had passed when men lived for the state. They

The change in the ideals of the Greeks

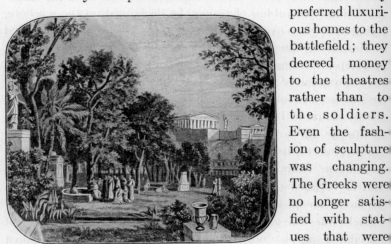

THE GARDEN OF AN ATHENIAN NOBLE

preferred luxurious homes to the battlefield; they decreed money to the theatres rather than to the soldiers. Even the fashion of sculpture was changing. The Greeks were no longer satisfied with statues that were strong and bold, they must be gentle and graceful. The most famous sculptor

Praxiteles, fourth century B. C.

of the time was Prax-it′el-es. His Aphrodite, made for a temple at Cnidus, was the first image of a woman who was not only beautiful but looked as if she could think and feel. The people of Cnidus were so proud of it that when a king offered to pay the large debt of the place if they would let him have it, they refused. Many of the Greek statues are known only through copies, but we have the original of Praxiteles's Hermes with the infant

Dionysus, which has felt the touch of the master's own chisel. These works are wonderfully beautiful, but just at that time the Athenians ought to have been thinking of their state rather than of statues. All the efforts of Demosthenes, however, were of little avail. Philip went on with his conquests in the north, and soon an opportunity presented itself for him to gain a footing in Greece and appear, not as the ruler of a rude, barbaric people, but as the protector of the rights of Apollo. The Pho'ci-ans had not always been careful of Apollo's claims. More than two hundred years earlier they had been punished by the Delphian amphictyony for interfering with people on their way to Delphi. Now the descendants of those same Phocians took possession of land that had been set apart for Apollo, and even stole some of the treasures from his temple. The amphictyony was no longer

strong enough to punish them and appealed to Philip. This was like inviting a cat to decide a question between two mice. Philip punished the Phocians, and the amphictyony gave him their votes in the amphictyonic council, and decreed that he should preside at the games held at Delphi. He was now the defender of

HERMES WITH THE INFANT DIONYSUS
(Discovered in 1877 at Olympia)

Demosthenes fails to arouse the Athenians

Philip becomes the champion of Apollo

Apollo; and if he could make it appear that any act of a Grecian state was a wrong to the god, he had a right to punish that state.

Philip's plans were progressing finely. His next step was to try to seize Byzantium. This did arouse the Athenians, for they by no means wished to be shut off again from the grain of the countries about the Euxine. They helped the people of Byzantium, and Philip withdrew his troops. He did not object especially to doing this, for he had a friend in Athens who was smoothing the way for him in another direction. This was the orator

Æschines

ÆSCHINES
(In the Museum at Naples)

Æs'chi-nes, the speaker who stood next to Demosthenes in eloquence. Philip kept well-paid servants and spies in the various states of Greece, and it is thought that Æschines was one of them. He persuaded the Athenians that the Phocians again deserved punishment for using some land sacred to Apollo. This was done merely to bring about an appeal to Philip, and Philip came promptly. But once in Phocis, he was in no haste to protect the property of Apollo. Instead of that, he took possession of a town convenient to both Athens and Bœotia, and fortified it.

Then there was no need of any brilliant oratory to make the Athenians see their danger. They were ready to do anything, to follow any one. "Make ready to withstand a siege," advised Demosthenes, "and get the help of Thebes." They obeyed without a murmur, and Thebes became

The battle of Chæronea, 338 B. C.

their ally. At Chær-o-ne'a in Bœotia the armies met, the best armies in the world. There was a terrible battle; and when it had come to an end, Philip of Macedonia was master of Greece.

Thebes and Athens had been the chief states in the league against him; how would he treat them? It was his opportunity to show once for all that he could be either severe or merciful, and Philip never neglected an opportunity. To Thebes he showed severity. He made her pay ransom for even the dead bodies of her soldiers; he freed the little towns of Bœotia from her rule; and he placed a garrison of Macedonians in her citadel. To Athens he showed mercy. He gave back her prisoners without ransom. He honored her dead with funeral rites, and then sent their bones to Athens under escort of his own son, Alexander. He retained some of her more distant possessions, but left her Attica, and even enlarged it by adding a little town on the Bœotian boundary which had long been a bone of contention between Athens and Thebes. *The severity and the mercy of Philip*

Not long after the battle of Chæronea, Philip requested the Grecian states to send representatives to a congress to be held at Corinth. First, a kind of union of states was formed, with Macedonia for its head. Then Philip laid before the council the real business of the meeting. It was to ask their aid in an expedition which had no less an object than the conquest of Persia. *Philip forms a union of states*

Philip was a shrewd man. He had shown the Grecian states that he was their master, but before they had time to attempt a revolt or even to realize their fall, he begged for their aid in an expedition which was to add to his glory, to be sure, but which would also avenge what they had suffered from the invasion of Xerxes. Of course they could hardly refuse whatever their conqueror chose to ask, but this was a most tempting expedition. The riches of Asia lay within their grasp. They had only to fol- *His plan of conquest* low the man who had shown himself capable of being a wise and successful leader. An offer of wealth and triumph and revenge

was enough to dazzle any nation. And this was no visionary, impossible scheme; the retreat of the Ten Thousand had shown what a feeble creature the clumsy, overgrown empire of Persia had become. They forgot that they had lost their independence, that they were a conquered people; they forgot everything except the expedition into Asia. All Greece began to make ready. Ships were built, supplies stored, arms and engines of war were prepared. Some of the troops had already started when Philip invited the Greek states to send representatives to the wedding of his daughter. The festivities were well under way. There was a magnificent banquet with all the rarities that the resources of the greatest king in the world could bring together. Then the guests, all aglow with handsome raiment and glittering with jewels, went from the banquet hall to the theatre. A long procession of Macedonians marched before their view, displaying the treasures of the kingdom. The last were the images of the twelve great gods. Some of the guests trembled at the impiety when they saw that a thirteenth had been added, the image of the king. Behind them walked the conqueror. He wore a wreath on his head and robes of flowing white. After him came his son Alexander and the bridegroom. The multitude shouted their applause. "Philip! Philip!" they cried; "great is Philip of Macedonia!"

PHILIP OF MACEDONIA
(From a coin)

In the midst of the rejoicing, there was one little gleam of the sword of an assassin, and the king lay dead.

SUMMARY

Macedonia was a rude country. Philip planned to make it strong. He formed the best army in the world. He improved upon the famous Theban phalanx.

Athens had been treating her allied cities as she had treated those of the Delian League. They revolted, and the Social War followed.

Demosthenes, after great efforts, had become a wonderful orator; but even his Philippics could not arouse the Athenians to their danger.

The Greeks no longer lived for the state. They preferred ease to battle. Even sculpture, as shown by the work of Praxiteles, had become graceful rather than strong.

At the request of the Delphian amphictyony Philip punished the Phocians, and was chosen to preside at the games held at Delphi. The orator Æschines brought about a second appeal to Philip by persuading the Athenians that the Phocians again deserved punishment.

Philip fortified a town near Athens and Bœotia.

The Athenians saw their danger too late. Philip's victory at Chæronea made him master of Greece.

Philip showed severity to Thebes and mercy to Athens. He formed a union of states with Macedonia for its head. Then he asked them to help him conquer Persia. They agreed with enthusiasm; then came the sudden death of Philip.

SUGGESTIONS FOR WRITTEN WORK

Philip tells what he learned as a boy in Thebes.

Demosthenes tells his actor friend how hard he has tried to become an orator.

Philip asks the Greeks to help him conquer Persia.

XX

ALEXANDER THE GREAT

WHEN the Greeks heard of the death of Philip and knew that a young man of twenty was on the throne, they were delighted.

"Greece will again be free!"

"Greece will again be free!" they said jubilantly. They would not have been so sure of their freedom if they had known what kind of youth it was who had become their ruler. They did know that at the battle of Chæronea, two years before, he had led the phalanx which had overcome the best troops of the Thebans. "But that was nothing," they said; "the oldest and most skillful generals were grouped around him to make sure that all went well." They might have guessed that he was no weakling if they had heard how, when he was a mere child, he had received some Persian ambassadors in his father's absence. They met him with proper deference, of course, but they expected him to talk like any other child. Behold, the little boy began to question them about their country. "What sort of man is your

Alexander's remarkable boyhood

king?" he asked. "How does he treat his enemies? Why is Persia strong? Is it because she has much gold or a large army?" The Persians gazed at him in wonder, and said to one another, "Philip is nothing compared with that boy." Another story told of him is about his taming the famous horse Bu-ceph′a-lus. It had been brought to his father for trial, but it had snorted and bitten and kicked and Philip had ordered it taken away. Then the boy Alexander cried, "What a horse they are losing for want of skill and spirit to manage him!" "Young man," retorted his father, "you find fault with your elders as if you could manage He tames the horse better." "And I certainly could," the prince declared Bucephalus boldly. "If you fail, what forfeit will you pay?" "The price of the horse." Probably the boy of ten or twelve years was no wiser in managing horses than the grooms, but he had noticed that they were leading the animal away from the sun and that his own moving shadow was startling and annoying him. Alexander turned the head of the horse toward the sun, stroked him and spoke to him gently, then sprang upon his back. The courtiers and the king had been amused at the boy's boldness, but now they were alarmed. Alexander, however, kept his seat, and after letting the horse prance and gallop as much as he would, rode up to the king. The father

ALEXANDER
(From a bust found in Tivoli, Italy, in 1779)

wept for joy. "Seek another empire, my son," he said, "for that which I shall leave you is not worthy of you."

Philip had provided tutors for his son, but he saw now that he had a boy to deal with who would not be satisfied with any ordinary teachers. The most famous philosopher of the day Aristotle, was Ar'is-tot-le. He was a Macedonian, but had long been a stu- fourth cen- tury B.C. dent in the school of Plato in Athens. To him Philip sent the following letter: —

"Be informed that I have a son, and that I am thankful to the gods, not so much for his birth as that he was born in the same age with you; for if you will undertake the charge of his education, I assure myself that he will become worthy of his father, and of the kingdom which he will inherit."

So it was that Aristotle became the teacher of the boy Alexander, and remained with him for at least three years, and possibly until he became king. Philip gave him a princely reward, for he rebuilt the philosopher's birthplace, the city of Sta-gi′ra, which he had once destroyed, and brought back the inhabitants, who had either fled or been sold as slaves. Aristotle liked to talk with his pupils while they were walking about together; so for a schoolroom Philip made ready a large and beautiful garden with seats of stone and cool, shady paths. Alexander not only liked philosophy, but he enjoyed reading the old plays and histories, and used to send long distances for them. Most of all, he loved Homer. His mother often told him he was descended from Achilles, the hero of the Iliad; and when he was a small boy, he was delighted to have one of his tutors address him as Achilles. Philip saw that his son could be trusted, and when he went to Byzantium he left the kingdom in the hands of the boy of sixteen. On his return he was amused and not at all displeased to hear the Macedonians call him "the *general*," but speak of his son as "the *king*."

He becomes the teacher of Alexander

Such was the young man who was now ruler of Macedonia and all Greece. Demosthenes called him a "boy"; but much trouble would have been saved if all his subjects had known what an unusual boy he was. Some of them, the wild mountaineers, thought this an excellent time to throw off the royal authority; but Alexander marched against them without a moment's delay. He found that he would have to clamber up a difficult

Alexander subdues the mountaineers

mountain road at whose top stood the rebels with heavy wagons ready to be rolled down upon him. It needed more than a few wagons to halt this quick-witted young commander. He ordered his troops to separate, leaving a clear path in the centre for the wagons. Where the road was too narrow for this, he had his men lie on the ground, holding their shields over their heads. The wagons rolled down slowly, then came faster and faster, struck the shields with a clatter and a crash, but went over them as if on a well-paved roadway, and tumbled harmlessly down the steep. It was not long before the rebels thought it best to surrender.

He shows his quick wit

GREEK SHIELD

Some of the states of Greece also had supposed that the death of Philip would give them a good opportunity for a revolt, but Alexander made a quick march into Thessaly. A mountain was in his way, but he cut steps up the precipices and pushed on. The states yielded, and now Demosthenes called him a "stripling." While Alexander was among the mountain tribes, a rumor arose that he was dead. Thebes and her friends thought that now if ever she could get rid of her Macedonian garrison. "I will show Demosthenes before the walls of Athens that I am a man," declared Alexander, and marched to the south. Thebes would not surrender until she was forced to yield. Athens had sent arms to the Thebans, but she did not attempt to resist a commander who could march at the rate of twenty miles a day through a wild and rugged country and over jagged mountain-ridges. "What shall be the punishment of Thebes?" Alexander asked the congress of states at Corinth. Either because they were afraid of him, or because Thebes had many enemies among them, they decreed that she should be destroyed.

Thebes revolts and is destroyed

The walls were razed and every house torn down save one, the old home of the poet Pindar. Even in the midst of warfare, Alexander still loved the old Greek poetry and remembered the honor due to the poet. Pindar's descendants, too, were safe, though thirty thousand Theban citizens were sold into slavery. The Theban lands were divided among the smaller towns of Bœotia.

There is a tradition that the philosopher Di-og'e-nes was then living in Corinth, and that Alexander had a curiosity to see him, which is not strange if half the stories told of Diogenes are true. One is that he was once seen in broad daylight carrying a lantern and apparently searching for something. "What are you looking for?" he was asked, and he replied, "An honest man." Another story is that when Plato was giving an elaborate dinner, Diogenes pressed his way in and walked over the

Salvator

DIOGENES LOOKING FOR AN HONEST MAN

carpets with bare and muddy feet. "Thus I trample on the pride of Plato," he growled. "But with greater pride, O Diogenes," Plato responded. When the king and his retinue drew near, Diogenes was lying in the sun and hardly took the trouble even to glance at the ruler of

his country. "Is there anything in which I can serve you?" Diogenes's
asked Alexander. The ungrateful philosopher replied, "Only reception of
stand out of my sunshine." The courtiers laughed, but Alexan-

der said thoughtfully,
"If I were not Alex-
ander, I would be
Diogenes."

He *was* Alexander
however, and he was
even more ambitious
of conquest than his
father had been. Two
years had passed since
the death of Philip.
Macedonia was quiet,
Greece was subdued.
There was no reason
why he should not set
out on the expedition
whose object was to

ALEXANDER AND DIOGENES   *Puget*

avenge the invasion of Xerxes, to conquer the kingdom of Persia, and to get the control of all Asia. He did not make the The begin-
mistake of Xerxes and assemble an army so large that it was invasion of
difficult to feed and move it; he led across the Hellespont only Persia, 334
between thirty-five and thirty-eight thousand men, but they had B. C.
been trained and drilled until they were almost invincible. In all
his preparations for the invasion Alexander had not forgotten
that he was a descendant of Achilles, and he went first to the
site of Troy, to pay honor to his ancestor. He offered a sacrifice
to Athene and hung a wreath on the pillar of Achilles's tomb.

"He was a happy man," declared the king, "in that he found a faithful friend while he lived, and such a herald as Homer to set forth his praise."

If Alexander did not have a Homer to set forth his praise, he had at least the most celebrated painter of ancient times to paint his portrait, and, moreover, he carried his painter to Asia with him. This was A-pel′les, and it is said that Alexander was so pleased with his work that he was unwilling to be painted by any one else. Apelles was quite as independent as the king himself, and, if we may trust the old stories, was far less courteous than his monarch. It is said that, when another artist was boasting of his rapid work, Apelles retorted, "The wonder is that you do not produce more of such stuff in the time." Another story is that he thanked a shoemaker most cordially for pointing out a mistake in a shoe latchet in one of his paintings. The man was so elated at having his advice accepted by the great Apelles that he went on to make more criticisms. Then Apelles said disdainfully, "Stick to your last, cobbler, stick to your last."

Of course the king of the Persians, Darius III, had heard what Alexander was about, and he had brought a great army to Asia Minor. The proper place to meet the audacious young man was at the Hellespont, the very entrance to Asia. Therefore, when Alexander came to the little river Gra-ni′cus, he saw the farther bank crowded with Persian soldiers. The river was apparently deep and swift, and the banks were as slippery as they were steep. The Macedonian officers objected to crossing at once; they said it was too late in the day, and, moreover, it was the wrong month, and they would surely be unlucky. But Alexander plunged into the river, and at his word the cavalry followed the great white plumes on his crest. Up the slimy bank they clam-

Apelles *(margin note)*

The crossing of the Gra-nicus *(margin note)*

bered, full in the face of the storm of Persian arrows. Meanwhile the phalanx was crossing the river, and after that came the infantry. Alexander won the day. Of the spoils of this, his first victory in Asia, he made many presents. First of all, however, he ordered a brazen statue to be made in honor of every man who

The victory at the Granicus

PASSAGE OF THE GRANICUS

had fallen in the battle. He gave lavish gifts to the Greeks, and to the Athenians, who seemed to be his favorites, he sent a special present of three hundred shields. To his mother at home in Mace-

Alexander sends gifts to the Greeks

donia, he dispatched the purple furnishings and the gold and silver dishes that were found in large numbers in the tents of the Persians.

He cuts the Gordian knot

Alexander marched south, followed the line of the coast a little way, then marched north to Phryg′i-a, taking cities as he went. Not much real warfare was necessary, for most of the cities near the coast surrendered promptly when they heard of his approach. In one of the temples of Gor′-di-um in Phrygia he found a celebrated knot, made of cords cut from the bark of a tree. There was an ancient prophecy that the empire of the world would fall to the man who could untie that knot. Many had tried their luck, but it was so cunningly tangled and twisted that no one had succeeded. Alexander, too, tried for a little while, then drew his sword and cut it. That is why, when

ALEXANDER AT THE BATTLE OF THE GRANICUS
(Bronze statue found at Herculaneum)

one has discovered a short, bold way out of a difficulty, he is said to have "cut the Gordian knot."

The victory at Issus, 333 B. C.

Toward the sea went Alexander and his men again, zigzagging through Asia Minor. At Is′sus he met the hosts of the Persians, who still thought that an army was sure of victory if it was only large enough. But they certainly learned better at Issus. Darius had unwisely allowed Alexander to meet him on a narrow plain where there was no room for his hosts. The Persians fled, their king taking the lead. Darius threw away his shield, his bow, his purple mantle, and even sprang from the royal chariot and leaped upon the back of a horse in order to get away faster. No one but the king had a right to give orders, and the whole Persian army tumbled over one another in their wild scramble to escape.

After the battle a most exquisite golden casket was brought to Alexander from the spoils of Darius. "What is most worthy to put into it?" he asked his friends. They proposed one thing and another, but the king shook his head. At last he said, "It

The golden casket

ALEXANDER AND DARIUS IN BATTLE
(From a mosaic in the Museum at Naples)

is the Iliad that most deserves a case like this." Darius's mother and family had been captured by the Macedonians. Alexander sent a message to them that they had nothing to fear from him, and treated them with the utmost courtesy and thoughtfulness. Darius wished to ransom them and offered his alliance; but Alexander bade the Persian monarch address him "not as an equal, but as lord of Asia," and he should have whatever he chose to ask.

Alexander's courtesy to royal captives

Where a city was situated or how it was defended seemed to

make little difference to this young conqueror. Tyre was on an island, but he soon made the island into a part of the mainland by building a causeway with vast mounds of earth from which

The capture of Tyre and Gaza

he could attack it with his engines of war. After Tyre had fallen, nearly all the cities of the country east of the Mediterranean surrendered, but he had to fight for Ga'za. From that city he sent to a former tutor of his great quantities of frankincense and myrrh. It seemed that when he was a boy the tutor had told him not to burn incense by handfuls until he had conquered the country where spices grew. Now he wrote, "I have sent you frankincense and myrrh in abundance, that you may no longer be a churl to the gods."

EGYPTIAN KING IN
WAR DRESS

Thus far Alexander had only begun his invasion. He had planned to go far, far to the eastward; but he meant to make sure that no enemies were left behind him. This was why he had marched back and forth through Asia Minor until he was certain that there would be no opposition in that part of the land. Before he struck out for the east, however, he wanted to make sure of Egypt, and thither he marched. Egypt rejoiced in the hope of being free from Persia. The Egyptians threw their gates wide open and came in throngs to bid him welcome. Near the mouth of the Nile he chose a site for a city, Al-ex-an'dri-a, to which goods from the east and from the west might be

Alexandria is founded

brought. He ordered his men to draw a line on the black soil, marking out the plan of the place. They had no chalk, and so they marked it out with flour. Suddenly, a cloud of birds alighted on the new city and ate up the flour. Alexander was troubled, fearing this might signify ill luck; but the soothsayers

said, "No, this is a sign that the city will be blest
with such plenty as to furnish a supply to those
that shall repair to it from other nations," and the king was comforted.

Meanwhile Darius had been
gathering men from the north,
south, east, and west to oppose
the invader. The best of them
were a number of Greeks whom
he had hired. He had also fifteen elephants and two hundred
scythed chariots, savage-looking
vehicles with sword-blades stretch-
ing out from the yoke and the
hubs of the wheels. The two

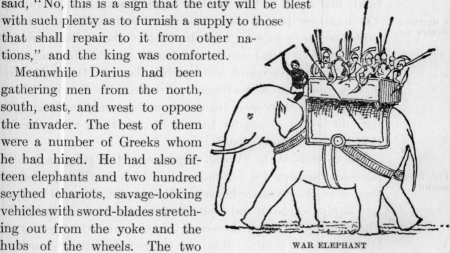

WAR ELEPHANT

armies met at Ar-be′la. The evening before the battle one of The battle
Alexander's generals proposed to him to attack the Persians in of Arbela,
the night. "Persian armies are almost helpless at night," he 331 B. C.

SCYTHED CHARIOT

urged. But Alexander was too proud to do this. "I will not
steal a victory," he replied; "I can beat Darius by open day-

light, and I will." And he did. Again Darius led the retreat.

The fugitives were so many and raised such a dust that in the confusion he escaped. For this battle Darius had brought together the greatest number of troops possible, had managed them as well as he could, and had been beaten. He could never do any more than he had done to drive out the Greeks. Therefore, although there were many long marches and no little fighting still before Alexander, his victory at Arbela really decided that Persia was in his hands.

The capitals of the Persian empire were Bab'y-lon and Su'sa.

Alexander expected a determined resistance in these places, for they were the treasure houses of the empire. Instead of that, the satraps came to meet him bearing the keys of the gates. The citizens scattered flowers in his way and thronged about him to offer their gifts. When he entered the cities, his wildest dreams of wealth came true; for in Susa alone there was more than $57,000,000, and in Per-sep'o-lis, his next conquest, there was more than three times as much.

Before he came to Persepolis he saw a pitiful sight: hundreds of Greek captives, some of whom had lost a leg, some an arm or an eye, and some who had suffered so severely that they were utterly helpless. This was the work of the Persians. Many of these captives had been kept in Persia for years. Tears came into Alexander's eyes and he urged them to return to Greece. "I will send you home," he said, "and see that you are well cared for as long as you live." But they told him they could not bear to return to their friends in such condition. Then he gave them land and slaves and many cattle. And yet, after the siege of Tyre, this sympathetic monarch had hanged two thousand men; and after the surrender of Gaza he had pierced with brazen rings the feet of the town's brave defender, tied him to a chariot, and dragged Alexander's cruelty him about, still living, in view of the army. So it was that Achilles had treated the body of his enemy Hector at Troy, he declared. It was a pity that from the Iliad in the golden casket he had learned no better lesson. After the overthrow of Persepolis, he gave the town to his soldiers to pillage. He slew the men of the city and sold the women as slaves. The destruction of Athens was avenged.

The first object of Alexander now was to capture Darius. The Persian king was fleeing, but he was really a prisoner in the hands of his own general, Bes'sus. Some of the Persians were planning to make Bessus king; but unless he could keep Darius as his prisoner, others would always have it in their power to plot to restore him to the throne. They were especially anxious that he should not fall into the hands of Alexander alive. When, The death of Darius therefore, they found that Alexander was at hand, and that they could not escape and take Darius with them, the treacherous Bessus and his friends hurled their javelins at him and left him for dead. It is said that a Macedonian soldier found him just alive, and that he expressed his gratitude to Alexander for having treated his wife and family so kindly. "Tell him I gave him my hand," he said. Alexander threw his own mantle over the body of the king and gave him a funeral with royal honors.

Alexander was master of the Persian empire, but he seemed to be seized with nothing less than a frenzy for conquest. Onward Alexander's frenzy for conquest he went with his invincible army, — north toward the Caspian Sea, south toward the Arabian, north again, winding and turning and zigzagging from the country far north of the Hindu-Kush Mountains down to India and the mouth of the Indus. He planned to go on and on to the most distant east; to make an expedition against Arabia by sea; to go far to the westward and conquer Italy, Spain, and northern Africa; in short, to unite the world in one vast empire of which he was to be the ruler.

Death of Alexander, 323 B. C.

He returned to Babylon to meet his new troops and vessels. The preparations were all made and he was on the point of starting, when he was suddenly taken ill and died.

Piloty

DEATH OF ALEXANDER

The exploits of Alexander

Alexander was thirty-two years of age. He had been on the throne for twelve years. In that time he had given peace to Macedonia and to Greece, he had destroyed cities and built cities, eighteen of them named for himself, and one for Bucephalus; he had made such marches and won such victories as no general had ever dreamed of accomplishing; he had ended the enmity between Persia and Greece, and he had gained an empire.

But what was to become of the empire? When Alexander lay dying, he was asked to whom he left his authority. "To the most worthy," he replied, and gave his ring to one of his generals named Per-dic'cas. No one but Alexander himself, however, could have held together the enormous empire. After many years of fighting and plotting, of confusion, uproar and violence, the mighty domain was broken into three parts, — Asia, Egypt, and Macedonia. Asia was governed by descendants of one of Alexander's generals, but one portion of it after another became a separate kingdom, until little but Syria and the lands lying immediately to the eastward of it remained united. A new power was rising in the west, the Roman, and Alexander's Asiatic possessions fell into the hands of Rome.

The breaking up of the empire

Egypt was ruled by another of Alexander's generals named Ptol'e-my. He made the country a naval power. He founded the famous Alexandrian Library; he invited large numbers of learned men and artists and poets to make Egypt their home; and he gave them most generous rewards. The line of Ptolemy ruled in Egypt for three centuries, but finally Egypt, too, fell into the hands of the Romans.

The fate of Egypt

Macedonia was supposed to govern Greece, but Greece was by no means a quiet subject. As soon as the Greeks heard of the death of Alexander, they followed the lead of Demosthenes and tried to resist the Macedonian rule. They were not successful, and Demosthenes fled to a shrine of Poseidon on a little island just off the coast of Argolis. He was pursued even into the temple. "Give me but a few minutes," he asked, "that I may write a letter." The officer granted his request. He began to write, then bit the top of his reed as if thinking. He threw a fold of his mantle over his head and neither spoke nor moved. The

Death of Demosthenes, 322 B. C.

soldiers drew aside the cloak and saw that the great orator was dying. His reed had been filled with poison, and he had taken

it, preferring to die rather than to be a prisoner in the hands of his enemies.

The Roman conquest

After a time the Greeks formed two leagues, but they could not agree, and therefore they had no power to resist the Romans. Both Macedonia and Greece became only parts of the Roman Empire. So it was that before the coming of Christ the

DEATH OF DEMOSTHENES

vast possessions of Alexander had become provinces of Rome.

What Greece did for the world

So ends the history of ancient Greece, the story of a people who, whatever were their faults, loved beauty and learning and free-dom. Nothing has ever sur-passed the art of Greece, her literature, or her language. He who would discover per-fection in art must go to her lifelike statues,

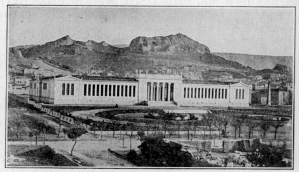

NATIONAL MUSEUM, ATHENS
(Where many art treasures of the ancient Greeks are kept)

her peerless edifices. He who would find in literature what is simple and grand and true and noble and eloquent, must read the writings of her poets and orators and historians and philosophers. He who would select a tongue in which every shade of thought and feeling may find adequate utterance must fix upon that of the Greeks. So it is that Greece, her statues shattered, *The immortality of Greece* her temples in ruins, much of her noblest literature vanished or known but in fragments, her language spoken, in modern form, by only a few thousands, is still the conqueror of her conquerors, — is still "immortal Greece."

SUMMARY

Alexander's remarkable boyhood.

After coming to the throne, Alexander subdued the mountaineers, made conquests in Thessaly, and overcame the Thebans. There is a tradition that he visited Diogenes.

Alexander invaded Persia. The painter Apelles went with him. Alexander was successful at the Granicus. He cut the Gordian knot, captured many cities, and at Issus routed the whole Persian army. He took nearly all the cities east of the Mediterranean and founded Alexandria in Egypt. He overcame Darius at Arbela, took Babylon and Susa and many other towns. Darius was slain by his own men. Alexander continued to make conquests throughout Asia, but died just as he was starting for the most distant east.

After years of confusion the empire of Alexander was broken into Asia, Egypt, and Macedonia.

Asia was governed by descendants of one of Alexander's generals, but the limits of the province soon narrowed to Syria and the lands lying immediately to the westward.

Egypt was ruled by a general named Ptolemy and his descendants. He made the country a naval power and a centre of art and learning.

Macedonia was supposed to rule Greece, but the Greeks resisted her rule.

Before the coming of Christ Alexander's vast possessions had all become provinces of Rome.

Nothing has surpassed the art, literature, and language of Greece.

SUGGESTIONS FOR WRITTEN WORK

What kind of boy was Alexander?

One of the rebellious mountaineers describes the descent of the wagons.

One of Alexander's soldiers describes the crossing of the Granicus.

SUGGESTIONS TO TEACHERS

IT is becoming generally recognized that the most elementary education is incomplete without some knowledge of the history of the Greek people, to whom the world has looked for guidance and inspiration in all the arts and sciences of civilization. History, literature, and art will always have many large gaps for the person who has not become appreciatively acquainted with Alexander, Homer, and the Parthenon. The Committee of Eight of the American ·Historical Association, in its Report on a Course of Study in History for Elementary Schools, says: —

" No people did more to begin the ways of living which we have and which our forefathers brought to America than the Greeks and Romans who lived about the shores of the Mediterranean when the Christian Era began. The aim of the topics selected from Greek and Roman history is to illustrate the characteristics of Greek and Roman life, and at the same time to interest the pupil in a few of the greatest memories which the Greeks and the Romans have left for all mankind to cherish."

The main consideration in the use of this book should be the desire to give pupils a permanent interest in the ancient Greek people — their immortal heroes, their great achievements, and their influence upon our civilization. The attitude of the child towards history is often determined in his first approach to the study of the history of any country, — whether he will regard it as a distasteful task to be thankfully dropped as soon as the last lesson is " recited," or whether he will enjoy reading and studying along similar lines in the future. Fortunately, the story of the Greek people, as told in this book, is absorbingly interesting to children, and with the proper degree of interest and enthusiasm on the part of the teacher every child who studies it will be eager to learn more about this wonderful people.

The book may be used either as a history text or as supplementary reading. Probably the best results will be obtained by having the children read an entire chapter through orally, discussing with the teacher points that need to be cleared up or emphasized, and getting the correct pronunciation of names; this to be followed by a re-reading of the chapter in a study period, with the summary at the end of the chapter before the pupil. The class will thus be prepared to relate the main incidents of the story. This may be done by asking a pupil to tell the story — or a definite part of it — to the class, the other pupils making any corrections or additions that may be needed at the close of his recitation.

May be used as a history text or as a reading book

The topics given at the close of each chapter, and many of the pictures in the book may very profitably be used in composition work. Thus, the description of the scene pictured on page 40, or a story based on the illustration on page 77, will give excellent results in composition, especially if the pupil is led to write or tell about these things because he becomes thoroughly interested in them.

Relation to composition work

In preparation for the reading of the book, pupils should locate Greece on the map of Europe in their geographies, and as they come to them they should connect the maps given in the book with the complete maps of Europe and Asia. It will be found helpful to have pupils quickly sketch outline maps upon the blackboard or upon paper and locate the important places and events being discussed. This is one of the surest ways of mastering the geography of a country, and it will prove an invaluable aid in the study of the book.

Geographical basis

INDEX

tyrant of, 105; prepares for a siege, 173;
helped by Alcibiades, 174; attack upon,
175-178.

Syr′i a, 237.

Tem′pe, Pass of, seen by Xerxes, 104;
abandoned by Greek troops, 107.

Temple, picture of ancient, 35.

"Ten Thousand Immortals," 101.

Theatre, description of, 139; at Epidaurus, picture of, 141.

Theatre of Dionysus, 139; restored, picture of, 140.

The′ban phalanx, improved upon by
Philip, 211.

The′bans, welcome the Athenians, 190;
deliver Thebes, 201.

Thebes, home of Œdipus, 9; overcome by
Athens, 71; Athens had defended Platæa from, 92; at the council of Corinth,
104-105; the home of Pindar, 120; Platæans feign to flee to, 158; joins union
against Sparta, 199; taken by the Spartans, 200; freed by Pelopidas, 201, 213;
Athenians jealous of, 202; becomes the
leader of Greece, 205; shows ingratitude
to Epaminondas, 207; cities turn against,
208; loses her power, 209, 210; Philip
at, 210; Philip learns about phalanx of,
211; aids Athens, 218; Philip's treat-
ment of, 219; rebels against Alexander
and is destroyed, 225-226.

The mis′to cles, the boy, 96; urges the
Athenians to build ships, 97-98; ex-
plains "wooden walls," 106; cuts messages upon the rocks, 111; forces a battle at Salamis, 113-114; treated unfairly,
118; wisdom of, 120; fortifies Athens,
121-123; tombstone found in ruins of
wall built by, picture of, 122; last years
of life of, 124-125; compared with Aristides, 126; banished, 130.

Ther mop′y læ, battle of, 107-110; Leonidas at, picture of, 109; Spartans at
Thebes different from those at, 201.

The se′um, picture of, 53.

The′seus, and the Minotaur, 6-8; before
King Minos, picture of, 6; slaying the

Minotaur, picture of, 7; possible origin
of the story of, 22; formed Attica, 53-
54.

Thes′pi ans, at Thermopylæ, 109.

Thes sa′li ans, 104.

Thes′sa ly, Xerxes sails to, 104; Alexander
in, 225.

Thirty Tyrants, the, rule of, 190; overthrown, 190; Critias, pupil of Socrates,
193.

Thrace, invaded by Darius, 88-89; again
invaded by him, 90; Doriscus in, 102;
invaded by Brasidas, 163-164; cities in,
lost by Athens, 169; Athens gets timber
from, 180; Alcibiades in, 185-186; invaded by Philip, 212.

Thra′cians, in Xerxes's army, 102; ask
the council of Corinth for aid, 106-107;
Alcibiades makes war against, 185.

"Throne of Xerxes," picture of, 100.

Thu cyd′i des, lived in time of Pericles,
143; picture of, 143; the boy, 144; style
of, 144; writes of siege of Platæa, 156;
describes fight at Pylos, 161; writes
history of the Peloponnesian War, 164-
165; writes of battle at Syracuse, 176;
selections from, copied by Demosthenes,
215.

Thyr′e a, 50.

Tis sa pher′nes, advised by Alcibiades,
181-182; found out by Spartans, 183;
Cyrus sent in place of, 186; Spartans
fight with, 199.

"Tortoise," the, picture of, 129.

Tower, with drawbridge and ram, picture
of, 157.

Treb′i zond, 198.

Tro′jans, in the Trojan War, 17-20.

Troy, fall of, 16-21; map of the siege of,
18; Athenian leader at, 105; visited
by Alexander, 227; Alexander imitates
Achilles at, 235.

Two-hundred yard dash, picture of, 76.

Tyrants, the rule of the, 83-84; overthrown, 85.

Tyre, captured by Alexander, 232; men
of, hanged, 234.

Tyr tæ′us, leads the Spartans, 48.

DUTRO
CALE

C.D.S.